hackyourhit.com

HACK YOUR HIT

**Free and cheap
marketing tips
for musicians**

Jay Frank

Futurehit, Inc.

Published by Futurehit, Inc., Nashville, Tennessee

Library of Congress Cataloging-in-Publication Data

Frank,Jay
        Hack Your Hit: Free and cheap marketing tips for musicians / Jay Frank
                p. cm.
        ISBN-13: 978-0-9846-8450-2
        ISBN-10:   0-9846-8450-6
        1.   Music Business. 2. Music technology.

Manufactured in the United States of America.

For every artist so they may survive life's daily hurdles

TABLE OF CONTENTS

Introduction   1

Talk To People   9

Twitter Search Your Fans   13

Twitter Search For New Fans   16

Be An Evangelist   21

Give It Away…But Get In Return   28

Carry A Signifier   32

Sell Your Music Everyplace You Can   35

Identify Fanbase By Fans   38

Craigslist   40

Identify Superfans   42

Nurture Superfans   46

The Second Stage Of The First Impression   49

Appear To Be Hitworthy   55

Pretty Girls   61

Google Search Band Name   63

Google Search Song Name   69

TABLE OF CONTENTS

Have A Gimmick   75

Google Alerts Of You And Your Competition   79

Don't Send Attachments   84

Always Promote Those That Promote You   88

Go Mobile   92

Boy, This Is A Lot To Manage   97

Comments   98

Read Derek Sivers' Book   101

Target Fans With Klout   103

Promote To Niche Sites   107

Watch Your Own Damn Video   110

Buy Your Own Damn Music   113

Gift Your Song   118

Get Paid To Buy Your Own Music   121

Create Your Own Music Hack Day   125

Have A Cool Merch Item   128

Interact With Everyone You Can   132

Unfollow Light Or Non-Followers   136

TABLE OF CONTENTS

Swap With Artists You Like   140

Release Music Often   144

Promote Photos   149

Contests   152

Target Friends Of Fans   155

Do A Show After The Show   159

Write Thank You Notes   162

Acknowledgements   167

INTRODUCTION

Just to start this book, I had to hack.

It's October 23, 2010, and I'm in Amsterdam speaking at the Amsterdam Dance Event about my book *Futurehit.DNA*. I had my plan set out well in advance. I would come in on Thursday and get my bearings. Friday, I would speak, schmooze and sell. Saturday morning, I would begin writing. This weekend in Amsterdam was key for me to get a good chunk of *Hack Your Hit* completed to get into your hands quickly. I had brought along my trusty MacBook Pro, which, at the exact moment I needed it to be trusted, failed. Within two sentences, the "s" key no longer worked.

I did all the things I could think of: I rebooted. I shut my laptop down entirely, let it rest, and started it again. I took off the "s" key, thinking I might be able to refit it, in case it had come off its mooring. All that did was subsequently disable the "x" key. Now, I was past frustrated; I was officially despondent. My whole plan for starting my book was flushed down the drain. Utter disaster!

With time on my hands, I went back to the ADE to continue schmoozing *Futurehit.DNA*, but truthfully my heart wasn't into it. I met my friend, Gary Smith from *Billboard* in the UK, and told him of my plight. Without even giving it a second thought, he suggested I go get a wireless keyboard. In fact, he knew of an Apple store only a few blocks away. And there it was: A hack.

Now, you probably don't think of getting a wireless keyboard as a hack, but it is. A hack, at its root, is a solution to a problem. In geek-speak vernacular, it's usually regarded as a breaking of the rules, and that's often true. Occasionally, it's illicitly breaking the rules. That ultimately gives hacking a very bad name. But most hackers are actually progressive people looking for solutions to the world's problems, discovering ways to move ideas forward. I didn't just have a solution to my problem, I had the mental uplift that allowed me to break through and start writing with minimal delay.

Usually, one hack begets another. So it was here.

I went down to the Eden Rembrandt Square hotel bar, where I met my friend Shamal Ranasinghe. Shamal is co-founder of Topspin, the service I use to sell my books online and to manage my customer database. Shamal is also a colleague from our days at Yahoo! Music, where we used to talk for hours about research and strategy. We were to meet for dinner, but neither of us was familiar with the city. The one recommendation I had would be impossible on a Saturday night. The one recommendation he had came from the concierge, not always the most trusted source, in my opinion. So we were stuck. What would we do?

I started telling Shamal how I had managed to hack for my book that morning, and how appropriate that experience was for a book about hacks. Without missing a beat, Shamal said, "We should hack dinner." How would we do that? Both of us instantly took to Twitter and asked people. Never mind that neither of us had friends in Amsterdam. We surely had friends who had *been* there. Indeed, within five minutes we had six recommendations and were searching our mobile phones for more information to make the right choice.

The Indonesian place that was our first choice was jammed and couldn't seat us for several hours, a sign that we made the right choice, but just too late. (We knew this place would be good because two people, who didn't know each other, recommended it.) We then soldiered on to our second choice, Castell. Totally different cuisine, and while near a very populated nightlife district, it was off the path enough to be somewhat hard to find. After a short wait surrounded by a colorful bar staff, we sat at a table with some locals, a French couple and an English couple and had some of the best barbequed steak we've ever eaten. (Thank you, Alan Kates.)

Yet again, another successful hack.

This hacking stuff is fun. And you know what? Once you put your mind to it, it truly is easy. Most hacking involves little more than taking time to think. An interesting dilemma in this digital era is that we are so constantly bombarded with information and things to grab our attention, we seldom feel as if we have time to do that. But when you do, you can usually solve your problem. And the benefit to you is that most people don't invest that time. In fact, given the number of artists out there trying to get their music heard, just taking the action of thinking about hacking probably places you in the top 10%. Actually making the hack? You're now in the top 1%.

The concept of this book came about after reading a fantastic book called *Hacking Work*, by Bill Jensen and Josh Klein. That book very neatly describes how one can take the basic concepts of hacking, in computer parlance, and apply them to the average corporate workplace. The book is not just filled with good ideas to get the job done it is also an inspiration.

Hack Your Hit does not guarantee that your song will be a hit. But it will provide you with tools and encouragements that can help you make your song a hit. The dialogue you have been hearing is true: It *is* possible for you to work completely within your own system, use your own creativity, and get a hit song despite corporate barriers.

At the same time, the "corporate barriers" (i.e., industry professionals) are effective for several reasons. They know the people and the process. They have the experience to know how, why and where different types of songs work. There are occasions where this "knowledge" works against them. The story of every label passing on the Beatles is one of them. But for all the hard knocks record labels take, the reality is they get it right a lot of the time.

So, because you probably don't have deep pockets, institutional knowledge and an address book bigger than your fan base, you're going to have to work extra hard. With that, it just makes sense to find hacks that make the process more direct, quicker and easier.

How possible is it? Let's look at the story of Auto-Tune The News.

This group of musicians/comedians had a unique concept: Take some local news reports and clips, put them through the Auto-Tune filter (the sound that "pitches up" bad singers, which T-Pain turned into a unique style) and make it a song. They placed these clips on their own YouTube channel and started building a base of fans. Each successive video increased their audience. When the time was right, they were primed to win.

That time came in late July 2010 when the group saw on TV a news report from a tough neighborhood in Alabama, where a man broke into a woman's apartment and attempted to rape her. What caught the attention of Auto-Tune The News was when her brother, Antoine Dodson, was interviewed for the story. In a very over-the-top style, Antoine looked right into the camera and directly addressed the intruder with phrases like, "We gonna find you!" and "So you better hide your kids, hide your wife..." and so on.

Auto-Tune The News went right into action, creating the "Bed Intruder Song." The song itself is a hack creation, though in today's Internet mashup world, it's seldom thought of that way. The hack is basically one of a "shoot first, ask questions later" mentality. They didn't contact anyone before putting it out. They let creativity dictate their direction, made the track and released it. It was only when they wanted to release it on iTunes that they needed to reach out to Antoine for permission to use his words. And for the record, as the composer of the lyrics, I understand that Antoine did receive 50% of the songwriting credit.

The end result was a YouTube and an iTunes smash. To my knowledge, it also became the first viral-only song without a record label or radio airplay to crack the *Billboard* Hot 100. While people have been saying since Napster in 2000 that an unsigned artist could take over the charts, it wasn't until "Bed Intruder Song" in August 2010 that the "independent code" was finally hacked.

In three months, the song received millions of views on YouTube across several videos and sold hundreds of thousands of downloads. Dodson appeared on the *BET*

Awards and sold a lot of t-shirts on his own website. Auto-Tune The News also got a production deal with Comedy Central. Lots of winners all around.

For all the visible rapid success of "Bed Intruder Song," remember that it happened after Auto-Tune The News had sown seeds for two years. They learned through trial and error what types of video pieces would get them the most traffic. They cultivated a regular relationship with their audience. They slowly built and believed in what they were doing. I do not believe they were aiming for overnight success, but they were certainly prepared for that moment.

So while it's nice to hope for hacks to give you instant hits, the reality is most likely the opposite. If you study most "viral" songs, you'll find that for every one that happens within a matter of hours or days, there are many more that actually grew slowly, for weeks or months, before finally catching on.

The truth about hit songs is that gatekeepers always make them. The key difference today is that the gatekeepers are far more accessible by the average person, either by direct contact or by that viral network of friends. A friend of mine, Marc Edelstein, sent me and a couple of other buddies a link to the message board of a drumming website. About as niche on the 'net as you can get. Marc is not in the music business, but he knew that I, as someone who is, would respond to the rant of a tour manager on this website. I did, and quickly placed the link on my @futurehitdna Twitter account. From there, several people retweeted the link. One of those people caught the eyes of noted sociologist Richard Florida, author of the fantastic books *Rise Of The Creative Class* and *Flight Of The Creative Class*. He then retweeted the link and reached a much larger audience, bringing more traffic to the site than that generated by the three-person chain that originally brought him the link. Why? Because he was a gatekeeper. For that matter, I was a gatekeeper, too.

"Bed Intruder Song" became a hit because many popular websites featured the video and attracted tens of thousands of eyeballs – gatekeepers all. Similarly, I would bet that iTunes, after seeing unexpected sales, featured the song in a few more places, making it easier to find. More gatekeepers. But this process is far different from earlier years of breaking songs.

Traditional "terrestrial" radio gatekeepers have sometimes used their ears, but most of the time they've relied on relationships, research consultants and various forms of enticement to decide which songs to play on the radio. Compounding the problem of tight playlists was that in the immediate years following deregulation of radio station ownership in 1996, the number of hits per year declined significantly owing to format consolidation and increased commercial loads.

Today, there are new avenues of access to listeners. Internet radio stations of all shapes and sizes exist to give a song a chance. There are bloggers who will write about a song they think will interest their readers, without even contacting anyone associated with the music. And where there were once only a dozen or so stations in a city, or a handful or even just one station that would fit the "sound" of your music, there are now thousands of blogs and radio sites that are all potential winners to play it.

Similarly, the gatekeepers of record sales were even worse. The pipeline was controlled by a few major labels, which had all the retail shelf space on virtual lockdown. The independents that did exist often lacked the juice to get sufficient copies into the stores. Even if they did, they might have lacked the juice to get paid for what was sold. Today, aggregators such as Tunecore and The Orchard make it much easier for you to get your music on the shelves and to be paid in a reasonable amount of time. Digital retailers have, in general, also taken a stronger interest in independent artists and they mine data to promote music that sells, regardless of the label behind it.

With these powerful new resources, the time has never been better for you to succeed in music … and never been worse. When I lecture on my first book, *Futurehit.DNA*, I often start with the staggering statistic that it's physically impossible for you to listen to even five percent of recorded music released every week. And that's presuming that you are actually listening every hour, every day, without any sleep. So grabbing someone's attention has never been harder. It's the trade-off for gaining easier access.

When a clampdown on corporate radio payola occurred in the mid-2000s, one expected that independent labels would rejoice that the barriers to entry would be lowered. Instead, many of them actually spoke out against the end of payola. Why? With payola, it may have been expensive to break a record at radio, but at least they knew what to do and the cost of entry. With payola stifled, and more records on an even playing field, the radio program directors (PDs) had too much choice. These PDs just didn't want to be bothered by the onslaught and instead stayed with what was most comfortable – music from major labels. After the economy soured in 2007, there was a big downturn in advertising on radio (resulting in lower rates and more "units" per hour), which certainly did not help matters. With ratings performance at a premium, these PDs felt they couldn't take chances, and that perceived risk was exactly what independents represented to them.

This selectivity process approximates what most Internet users go through with music. They are not like you or me. They are not obsessed with music. They do not read music blogs regularly and don't buy or stream a ton of music. In general, music comes to them virally, if at all. They tend to hear the music that's in front of their face. That narrows the playing field a lot.

So this book aims to help you cut through filters, limitations and other external forces and find the hacks that give you greater odds of success. Don't implement all these ideas at once, but the recommendations are, it's hoped, inspirational starting points. I would love nothing more than to have someone come up to me, say they read a certain chapter and tell me it sparked a new hack that was a variation of what I had discussed. To me, those are the best hacks.

A good hack can be complex, but it is often deceptively simple. With that in mind, I tried to contain the ideas in this book within short, punchy chapters. My goal is to get your brain working in as many creative ways as possible. The best hacks are based on how they're used in practice. Hackers aren't comfortable with just coming up with a path to a solution. That path must be tread on with regular success to achieve its greatest potential.

Of course, the best hacks are not all mine. I do my best to give credit where it's due for the best ideas that come my way. These people generally want to share their ideas so they can help more musicians, just as they were helped. Hacks are seldom created in a vacuum. They are almost always a collaborative process focused on identifying the best solution in the least amount of time.

And that brings me to the first hack. Let's dive in!

TALK TO PEOPLE

I know what you're thinking: "Too easy. Too obvious. And nothing apparently technological about it. I paid for this book and you're telling me to talk to people? *This* is worth the price of admission?"

Yes, because most people either do it incorrectly or don't do it at all.

It's amazing how many artists, whether because of their own ego or insecurity, fail to simply ask certain questions. There's no downside in asking. We may not know the answers. Our friends may not, either. But it's entirely possible that the friends of our friends do. The beauty of today's world is our interconnected lives. That's called networking. And that's the simplest hack.

When I first got into the music business, one of the key nuggets of advice given to me was to get to know as many people as possible. I was taught that the music business was driven much more by who you knew than what you knew. The truth is actually a balance of the two. However, that networked connection used to be protected by those who worked in the seats of music business power. The "friends of friends" seam was difficult to mine at best. Even if your friend did know someone to solve your problem, it was often difficult even to get him or her on the phone, let alone to get his or her attention. Now, those friends are all a post or message away. They can answer at their leisure and address at their own pace. Not a week goes by without someone I know reaching out to ask my assistance with a question or for a connection.

Those connections may occasionally be obvious, but usually they're not. It won't become apparent until the question is asked. Are you sitting there struggling with the idea of getting an app for your band online? Are you spending hours wading through websites, each offering to do the job at a different price? How much time is lost seeking that key bit of information you need that could have been spent actually making the app or promoting the music? Why not just send a message to your social networks asking for solid recommendations?

The key to successful hacks is saving time. When you're trying to grow your audience, you need to spend as much time as you possibly can actually doing it. Would you rather devote four hours to making new fans or to looking for a way to make an app and getting overwhelmed by the choices?

Chances are that the questions you're asking have already been asked thousands of times. There's no sense trying to solve a problem when someone else already has. That's poor time management, and none of us can afford that.

The first way to source the answer is to ask the people you know best: your parents, family and friends. Ask the bartender at your favorite club. Ask the person at the instrument store you frequent. Don't be shy. As a matter of fact, if this scares the living daylights out of you, stop reading this book and sell your guitar. Take that money and buy lottery tickets instead, as those offer you better odds for success than the music business. I'm not exaggerating. As you'll learn throughout this book, nearly all of the hacks to success require social skills. If you lack them, you have an extraordinarily low chance of music success.

Beyond the people you're in touch with on a regular basis, ask those in your social network. If I had been writing this book in 2007, I would likely have made joining a social network its own hack. Let's assume at this point that you have done the basics and signed up to Facebook, Twitter or Tumblr – even better, all three. Why? You need to be wherever people may find you. You wouldn't say, "I want to sell my music in WalMart and iTunes, but not Best Buy or Amazon," because you want to do as much business as possible. Same goes with the major social networks. Always remember, it's your job to reach people, not their job to reach you.

Let's also assume you've done that legwork and cultivated your social networks. Now's the time to ask them for help. If they're really a part of your network, they *want* to help. It doesn't matter if that network has 20 people or 20,000. Ask them all. The worst thing that could happen is that they don't have an answer; the best thing is that they do. No downside. So go ahead and ask.

But what if your family has no connections, and your social network was no help – what then? Ask the Internet. As with many things, it's all in how you ask and where you ask it.

First, try a Google search. If you're looking to create an app, don't just type "create an app." That will probably yield very poor results. Try "mobile app music artists develop." If you don't get the answer you need, just refine your search. The key is to be very specific. There's a good chance that many people have asked the question that you have, and it's likely that someone has already answered it.

But why stop at Google? There are thousands of video tutorials on YouTube about the very things you need to know.

It's also likely that someone has already asked the question on Twitter or Facebook and received a useful answer. Try http://openstatussearch.com or search.twitter .com. Again, the only downside is that you don't get the answer; the upside is that you do.

Then there are the answers sites. Whether it is Yahoo! Answers, Answers.com or Quora, there are countless people who have solved millions of problems, and those answers are just sitting there waiting to be found. And if those sites don't offer a solution to your problem, ask the question yourself, and see if the community comes up with the answer. If they do, then you'll also "pass it forward" for the next reader of this book that may have the same question.

In all, asking for advice is easier than ever. The aggregate time to go through these steps is probably no more than an hour or so. It's sure to be faster and more successful than spending many hours looking for an answer and failing to find it, or worse, trying ideas that have already been known to fail.

Never waste time. Every minute should be used productively to grow your musical career. Attempting to recreate solutions that already exist is probably the single biggest thing you could waste your time on. Don't do it. Just ask.

TWITTER SEARCH YOUR FANS

How often do you find new people who are fans of your band? And once you find them, what do you do with them? Maybe you get excited and say, "Wow, So-And-So is a fan of my band. I never knew that." Congratulations! You should celebrate that. But if you stop with that thought, you will not succeed.

The sad reality is that most people who like music don't want to take the time to become a fan, at least not in the strictest sense. They don't want to buy everything you put out. They don't want to attend a show. They don't want the t-shirt. But that doesn't mean that they won't.

Customer acquisition is usually the hardest part of any business. More precisely, getting someone to actually try a product, interact with it or visit a store is the most expensive part. Once someone does make the initial "entrance" and shows an inclination towards a product, the company has a much easier time establishing and then maintaining a relationship. If it isn't actually easier, it's certainly cheaper to keep the customers it already has. If a firm does do that successfully, it not only makes profits from that person, it has a higher likelihood of growing, because that customer is likely to be saying good things about it.

Whether you like it or not, if you are interested in having a hit with your music, your music is also a business. Perhaps you already have set up your artist venture as an LLC. Regardless, you need to view your music from a business perspective in order to succeed. Since we're a creative community, we get to call customer acquisition by the slightly sexier name of "growing a fan database," but it's the same thing. So we collect names through mailing lists at concerts, give away free downloads and try to attract people via voluntary signups on Facebook or Twitter.

That's all well and good, but what about all those people too lazy to sign up for your feeds? You may think it's easy, but the average person surfing the Web won't do it unless it's right in front of their face. Maybe that person is not inclined to "like" your band on Facebook because they're just not about that. Quite likely, taking that action may not even be in their peripheral vision. The reality is that the vast world of the Internet makes "liking" you a chore that most don't realize they "should" do.

It's up to you to get them to recognize and act on this chore. Fortunately, there are people who regularly advertise that they might want to be fans. You just have to look for them. That's where social network searches like Twitter Search, Open Status Search and "scraping" tools like Google Alerts come in handy.

All you need to do is search for yourself on a regular basis. It's not narcissistic; it's called "looking for your fans." Type in your artist name and see what comes up. It may produce nothing, but as you grow, you may find something. Maybe someone remarks, "Just discovered So-And-So on Pitchfork, and they're pretty good." Bam! Perhaps they said, "Heading out to the So-And-So show at the Roxy. Meet me there." Wham! Or perhaps they said, "Listening to So-And-So while cleaning the kitchen." Huzzah! Potential fans all.

But don't stop at searching for your band name. What about your songs? You'd hate to miss someone saying, "I really like that Cool-Lyric song." A lot of people hear songs and don't know who's singing them. I know, even with Internet music discovery sites showing the artist and song title right next to the song nearly every time, you'd still be surprised how many people have no idea what your name is. That takes hard work, even for artists with big hit songs. So, don't take anything for granted. Search your song names, including misspellings and variations. Search your album name. Search your lead singer's name. "Wow, I think Hot-Singer is hot." Another fan. Get 'em all.

Pay close attention to the ways people talk about you. If they misspell your name, recognize it and utilize it. Most artists have to deal with some form of mangled names, title and lyrics somewhere along the way. For months, when I saw search terms that brought people to my website for Futurehit.DNA, I noticed that a sizeable minority were looking at "Future Hit" rather than my preferred "Futurehit". Minor issue, I thought, because they were still getting to my site. But it took me awhile to realize that I needed to add "Future Hit" to my Google Alerts, along with "Futurehit." While doing this produced a lot of people who would not be leads, I did find fans I would have missed otherwise.

Once you identify these people, reach out to them. All of them. Friend them. Send them a tweet. Email them a free download link. Use every means you can to get to them. I mention bands regularly in my status updates. Know how many reach back out to me? About one in 50. Trust me, your connection will stick out; it will take you a good step closer to having a fan. The person may think, "Wow, that band noticed me." People like to be recognized, so recognize them.

But don't stop there. Every once in awhile, group all these new friends together and put them in a post. Say, "Thanks to all of our new fans," and list them. You like to be acknowledged. So do your fans.

Heck, why stop at status updates? Did you ever read a blog in which you were mentioned? Did that pop up on your Google Alerts? Sure it did. But did you then find out who wrote it? Research that person's Twitter name? Reach out to them on Facebook? You get my point.

These people are ADVERTISING to be your fan. They want to be heard. They want to be acknowledged that they're cool for knowing you. They want to be appreciated that they openly liked you. So do it.

TWITTER SEARCH FOR NEW FANS

How do you go about finding prospective fans? How do you make the most productive use of your time? And how do you do it without annoying everyone? Well, you have to be careful about the annoying part (that's all in your tone), but I can help you with the other stuff.

First, identify the artists you think appeal most to people who will also like your music. Begin by polling your fans about their musical choices. Let's not fool ourselves. Because it's often hard to pull people to where they want to be, go where your fans naturally are. There's a time and place to lead people, but at this point, you need people to lead.

Also, aside from polling your fans, make sure that you look at iTunes and Amazon sales of your music and see what the profile is there. Even if your sales are small, these sites will aggregate the artists that your buyers have bought the most. From that list, you might be able to pick up a few good artist ideas. It doesn't have to be perfect, it just needs to be a place to start.

Now that you have your list of artists that your fans like, cross off the three biggest acts. Going down those roads will be a waste of time, because *everyone* likes them! If people who like you also like U2, that obviously doesn't mean that U2 fans will automatically like you. It just means

U2 is so big that inevitably you will have a decent number of U2 fans. Also keep in mind that fans of these hugely popular bands tend not to be passionately open to new artists. Their tastes are so broad and mainstream that they may provide very little help to your career. There are exceptions to the rule, of course, but we're trying to save time. So cross those names off.

That still leaves you with a list of some good-sized bands. Find the three that you think inspire the most passionate response from their fans. You are focusing on finding those people who, should they like your music, will generate a fervor that is contagious. You want to get fans that are not only going to like you; they'll also tell all their friends about you.

How do you find these fans? There are many ways, but I like a site called Tweetreach. On this site, you can type in any subject and get a snapshot of the people who have been tweeting about that subject recently. It's mostly like Twitter search, but it contains a key difference.

In the right column of the Tweetreach results page is a list of impressions for each person. Tweetreach looks at the people tweeting about your chosen subject and calculates how many followers they have. This allows you to see the number of "impressions" each of their tweets can make. Naturally, you want to reach as many people as possible, so start with the top three people on that list. But before you contact them, make sure you double-check their tweets to ensure they're a good match. They may live in another country, which might not be a good target. They could also be mentioning the artist negatively. No sense reaching out to the person who does not fit your fan profile.

After you've identified three key prospects, your next move is to begin following them. This is a welcome gesture to show that, before you ask anything of them, you are adding yourself to their list of followers. If they turn out not to be interested in communicating, you can always unfollow them later. Wait a few days to see if they will follow you. If they do, you now have the perfect opening to reach out. Send them a tweet thanking them for the follow, and mention that you thought they might like your music. Send them a link to the most productive place you've found your music exposed: free download link, YouTube, Myspace...wherever you see the best results.

When you send your message, be very cordial. Remember, you hate spam, too, and the end user could regard your message that way. If they think it's spam, they may think your link is a virus and flag you to Twitter. If you make it personal (don't cut and paste), you are much more likely to get a response. Word it in a way that shows that you genuinely think their life would be better if they listened to your music. Don't solicit for sales. Don't hard sell *anything*. Just ask them to listen.

If you do get a response from your music, be sure to thank them. There's nothing worse than asking someone for something and then not acknowledging them. When you do, though, that's where you can start trading, because people like being noticed. At the end of the week, you might put their Twitter name on a post to thank them for being a new fan. In return, they will be more likely to tell their friends you acknowledged them.

All any of us want is to be noticed and recognized. As P.T. Barnum once said, "The first rule of success is to be noticed," and it works for you when you do it for others. Taking the time to show the world who these fans are means the world to prospective fans. It proves that you're not a machine, that you are real and that you care. All are key elements in building fans.

But only you know that you were just being strategic. You didn't go for the fan that had 100 friends. You went for the prospective fan with a few thousand friends. And that means when they return the favor, the impact is magnified that many times. If this person indeed mentions you, you will likely pick up a few followers who will also try out your music. This process takes time, so don't be discouraged. Also keep in mind that if you find a fan with a thousand followers, and only 10 people respond, that means you got a 1% response rate. In the Internet world (and even in direct mail), that's good. And if those 10 people like your music, awareness will begin to spread.

Unless these individuals are known media people of any type, they are also likely not getting hit up a lot to listen to a lot of bands. For the most part, a fan with fewer than 10,000 followers is pretty much under the radar. So they likely have not gotten a lot of emails directly from artists asking them to check out music. That's good for you because it increases the likelihood that you will get heard.

Not surprisingly, you want to pay attention to which fans generate a higher response rate. You want to spend your time with the tree that bears the most fruit. If Artist A fans tend to not respond, but Artist B fans do, then the answer is simple: Stop looking for fans of Artist A. Better to go to Artist C than keep banging your head against a brick wall. Also, when you send a link, always use a link shortener that tracks back, such as ow.ly or bit.ly. This way, you can measure how many people actually did follow through to hear your music.

The reason you want to limit yourself to the top three artists on the list is because you are looking for maximum impact. The lower you go, the more time you spend. If your artist has active fans, you should be able to run a Tweetreach report every day and see new prospects at the same level as your original batch. So rather than spending time dipping down to fans with fewer fans, just take your time and find more popular fans another day.

The other reason you want to focus on the top three is that you don't want to get a reputation as a spammer. In the worst-case scenario, you could get kicked off Twitter, which would obviously not be a good thing. Even if you don't get kicked off, you don't want people talking negatively about you. If you are very polite and selective, then even if people are not interested, they are likely to just ignore it. For this reason, don't keep hammering anyone for a response. They'll give it to you if they want to.

Using search tools for Twitter can be very effective to begin your road to viral growth. But it's a slow, deliberate and calculated process. Don't overdo it, and don't expect overnight success. Just let yourself grow, step by step, and a fan base will begin to emerge. Try it and see.

BE AN

EVANGELIST

How passionate are you about your music? Do you not only play it, but also live and breathe it? Do you feel the need to speak about it to everyone, everywhere? Do you talk about the music you create with a veritable reverence that suggests it is the most amazing thing to grace the planet? Do you do this for what seems like 24/7? If you don't, you might as well accept that music is your hobby and give up on the notion of having a hit. I'm not kidding. Give it up, buddy.

Now, I don't mean to be harsh or turn you off to reading the rest of the book. I'm only exposing you to the reality of the competition you're up against. If you don't have the passion, determination and stamina to work tirelessly on your own behalf, than you'll never make it in this business.

Of course, this is nothing new. Read artist interviews in *Rolling Stone* or any other music publication. Notice how they talk about new projects with uniform praise, even though two years later, they may acknowledge that the record was "not quite what they expected" in a subsequent interview in the same paper. Until artists achieve a superstar level, they probably give the same interview, with similar quotes, over and over again in music magazines, on TV shows, radio stations and blogs, and then repeated in numerous countries. Sometimes they do it on media days where multiple outlets gather in one spot, and the artist basically does the same short interview with the same talking points. Dozens of times. In one day.

They are media-trained evangelists.

The beautiful thing about our technological world, though, is that you don't have to wait for a PR person to set up a phalanx of interviews for you to be an evangelist. You can start today. Twitter can be your megaphone. Facebook can be your lamppost flyers. Your blog can be your sermons. But you must evangelize. Trust me, it works.

Do not just evangelize on the Internet. Evangelize to every person you meet, and get everyone you meet to do it, too. Use every opportunity to evangelize. Do it repeatedly. With the same people. Preachers are most effective when their message is repeated to the same crowd multiple times. Just as an effective chorus needs to repeat key phrases multiple times to create singability, so must your message.

When I blog about an important topic that I know the audience will find important, I do not just put out one blast on Twitter and hope for the best. I usually repost the article four times over two days. Each time I use a different headline, but I'm always pushing it. Why? I want to make sure all my fans are aware of the information I'm putting out, so I keep mentioning it. Even people who did not read it the first time might respond the second or third time. Maybe that later occasion feels more important. Maybe it was worded a bit better than the last time. I don't care why; I just want them to read it. I'm evangelizing something important. You'd better do the same.

Make your evangelism spread to others. Start with friends and family. After all, they're your biggest fans. Scott Swift, father of Taylor Swift, has a habit of always having Taylor's guitar picks in his pocket. If you have even a brief conversation with him, you will certainly leave with the latest design of Taylor's guitar pick. Even after she'd sold over 10 million records, he still handed out guitar picks. He's an evangelist.

In tech circles, it appears that evangelists are actually now a trend. During the first wave of Internet successes, it was about the partnership. Usually a creative type paired with a business type to build a successful venture. Think

Google's Sergey Brin and Larry Page. Think Yahoo's Jerry Yang and David Filo. Think YouTube's Chad Hurley, Steve Chen and Jawed Karim. Each rose to new heights in the 2000s via this new creative/business balance that served them well.

This decade appears to be about the solo entrepreneur. But dig deeper, and you'll realize it's not that they are solo, it's that they are evangelists. They're working tirelessly to make sure that you are aware of their services and will do anything to make sure they succeed. People such as Facebook's Mark Zuckerberg and Spotify's Daniel Ek seem to be everywhere, always talking up their services, and with good reason. They are passionate about what they're doing.

Let me tell you how one of my favorite entrepreneurs conquered the odds to succeed by evangelizing. My personal connection to him makes me admire him even more.

If you had to think of the brand-name example of an online radio service that personalizes its stream of music to your taste, what name would come up for you? You mean it's not LAUNCHcast? Back in 2005, the dominant name in Internet radio was indeed LAUNCHcast, owned by Yahoo!, I was proud to head the music programming team that powered this great service. We led ratings for listenership by a considerable margin, streaming more than a billion songs a month. Bright minds, including my friend Todd Beaupre, had worked tirelessly since 1999 to deliver a stream that conformed directly to the listener's tastes. It crowdsourced musical interests to deliver music based on what other fans of that music liked. It was musical nirvana for millions of people.

So, how did an independent company like Pandora (the name I presume you thought of when I asked the question) overtake a market-leading service backed by a big company? In this case, a lot of little factors added up, but in my opinion, the answer was in the passion of the company, manifested in its founder and evangelist, Tim Westergren.

In those early days, Pandora looked nice, but I can remember criticizing a lot of what it had to offer. Pandora was powered by the Music Genome Project, which had dozens of musicologists listen to every piece of music for key attributes that determined how a song sounded. It then matched that sound with similar songs. LAUNCHcast crowdsourced, with millions of people giving feedback on their musical tastes. Here, a handful of folks made opinions that determined your musical future. Was that markedly better than a radio station programmer?

In its initial days, Pandora acquired a decent, devoted following, but it was no threat. There appeared to be an overemphasis on independent artists. Recommendations were often obscure and odd, even if they may have been on the same sonic plane. After a few years, it appeared that Pandora was going to occupy little more than a comfortable niche.

Tim, however, made all the difference. A very approachable, nice guy, Tim made it his life's mission to spread the word about Pandora. He didn't just take to the Internet and spread his message. He took to the streets. Literally.

For months on end, Tim visited every city he could. He reached out to Pandora fans well in advance. When one occupies a cult niche, your base may be small, but it is passionate. So he sought them out, and arranged for meetups, often at coffeehouses that would be accessible to all. He didn't know what he would get. Would five people show up? Fifty? The turnout didn't matter as much as the evangelizing.

Tim met with various industry folks in each town. Maybe some local press, too. Then, he went to the meetup place. He discussed with the fans what they liked and didn't like, his plans and vision. He got them on board. He handed out free T-shirts. He took pictures of him with the crowd to post online.

The evangelism worked. Very quickly, these coffeehouses were packed to the rafters. People had trouble getting in to meet Tim. Word spread to the next town that you had to get there early. Fans brought friends who all wanted to be part of a happening. Pandora fans entered the room and saw that they were not alone. They found that more people were like them than they knew. They left talking about how cool Pandora was as a service *and* that the man running the show was also a great guy. So you had to listen, too.

All because Tim was an evangelist.

Now, Tim could have easily spent every day in his office working on building a better product. His day could have been sucked up talking to record labels in New York and Los Angeles, which he also did. He could have been cloned and sent others to meet with ad agencies in those cities and Chicago. But he somehow found the time to do those things, as well.

Coffeehouses, label meetings, ad agencies, auto manufacturers – he did that *and* kept a staff motivated back home in Oakland. And found investors. And fought for lower royalty rates so he could afford to grow the business and make up for the lower rates to labels with higher volume.

Jeez, how many hours a day did this guy work? Obviously, all of them. I'm sure he probably had many nights where he went back to wherever he was staying (likely a friends' couch or an affordable hotel to save money) at 11pm and dealt with emails from his staff, the labels and other fans around the world until the wee hours of the morning. Then got up early to finish the job, travel to the next city and do it all over again. When you're an evangelist, you don't just find the time. Time becomes irrelevant because it consumes you that fully. That's what you have to do.

My Amsterdam trip mentioned in the introduction was one of those evangelizing trips for me. Spreading the word on *Futurehit.DNA* has been my passion ever since I began writing it, but I have barely turned a profit on it. However, that's not as important to me as spreading the message the book offers, as I fully believe it holds the key to a more financially vibrant business that will secure my financial future. Evangelists have to have some blind faith. Heck, I used my vacation days from my primary job as Sr. VP of Music Strategy at CMT in order to work and evangelize this passion. If you have a day job, do you do that?

On this evangelical mission, I met up with my friend Laurence Tolhurst, an original member of the Cure, at an Indonesian restaurant with the rest of his band Levinhurst, which were touring Europe at the time. Somehow the subject came to vices, and I asked him what he thought my vice was. With barely a hesitation, he declared that my vice was that I am a workaholic. As an evangelist, I never think about it as a vice. I think of it as a lack of choice.

I'm writing this section on an airplane back from that Amsterdam trip. A candy-bar of a Hollywood movie that one only watches on planes is playing in the background. People on either side of me are sleeping. Me? I'm writing this book. On my day off. Because I have to evangelize.

There is a two-fold need for taking the evangelist approach. The first is the obvious one of turning people on to your music. Nobody can convince someone your music is great better than you can. You attempt to do this when you're onstage. You do it when you record your music. Why wouldn't you do it everywhere you go?

The other reason is for you to sense what your competition is like. Most of the successful artists I know are evangelists. Taylor Swift is the first artist I met who truly embraced this "new evangelistic" attitude and set the standard. In her first year as a recording artist, I saw her sign autographs for hours with a line that snaked around a venue. She smiled and was as gracious to the last person as to the first. One time, she performed at a corporate event I arranged. On the van ride from the airport to the event, she whipped out her laptop with her 3G web connection and started evangelizing to fans. She couldn't even waste the time in a 20-minute van ride. Evangelist.

You have to find your own way to evangelize. You can't force yourself to do things that feel uncomfortable. It has to be in your own style, because people can certainly see through a false front. However it works for you, do it and keep doing it.

If you think that you can go back to school and be a lawyer if this "music stuff" doesn't work out, you might as well just go to school now. The ones who succeed are the ones with blind vision to the future. They succeed because they have no other choice. If they fail, they will have nothing. This was true 20 years ago. But now, we're living in a land where there are over 100,000 "preachers" putting up pulpits all around you. Who does a fan choose to follow? Certainly not the one who does little to inspire the following.

I said it at the beginning, and I'll say it again. Be an evangelist for your music or forget the hit and just go home.

GIVE IT AWAY ...BUT GET IN RETURN

There's been a lot of scuttlebutt throughout the DIY music scene on whether or not you are supposed to give away your music. Does it add value, or does it make your music worthless? Does it build a fanbase? Encourage piracy? I actually have a pretty simple statement on what you're supposed to do with free downloads:

Give your music away...but never give it away.

It's basically a simple way of saying something obvious. Yes, you should give away your music for free. However, just as in any transaction in life, it should not be given away unless you get something in return. That something may not be a lot, but it should have meaning and value to you.

To quantify that, let's determine what the value is. If you're like most of us in the music business today, you're presuming the value is 99 cents. Therefore, it's tough to stomach the notion of giving away a bunch of downloads because, each time you do, a buck is taken from your pocket.

Let's deflate that fantasy bubble. First, you'd have to assume that whoever is getting the free download would have purchased it instead. The truth is, of course, that the overwhelming percentage would not. Money you were never going to get is not money lost.

Second, you have to think about what people are going to do with the download. Well, what do *you* do with the free downloads you get? How many do you listen to once and then forget? Maybe you leave them on your hard drive, or maybe you delete them. The reality is that the vast majority of free downloads will only be listened to once.

Now that we've established most downloads net one listen, how do we appraise the value of that one spin? Pandora, Spotify and YouTube have well-established rates of how much they pay for an individual play – a fraction of a penny. For the sake of discussion, we'll call it a quarter of a cent, unless you're well known with a lot of leverage. So, basically, your free download is worth $0.0025.

However, now that you view it this way, it's very easy to give up that quarter-cent. How many times do you pass over a penny on the street? Every time you pass over a penny on the street, it's like giving away four downloads of your song. No big deal.

While only some people listen to a song more than once, their value is much greater because that means they like it. And *that* usually means they're telling someone about it, which may well lead to a new fan who may pay 99 cents.

Here comes the best part. Even though we've placed an outrageously low value on the download, we still want to get something back. That something usually takes the form of information, which can have a value far greater than the quarter-cent. This can be viewed either by its potential use for future income or simply what you would get if you were buying a targeted contact list on the open market. Either way, you will definitely get more in return than you gave out for your song.

The easiest, most obvious piece of information to get is a person's email address. To prevent appearing as spam, you then send a link to the download in the form of an email. Topspin has a fantastic widget that can facilitate this for you. You will get few dummy emails, and you will have a list of people you know have received your music. It's pretty easy, it's the preferred method of most musicians, and it's effective.

If you're feeling ambitious, you can also ask recipients some general questions about themselves. How old are you? What's your ZIP code? How many Mötley Crüe concerts have you been to? Easy stuff. Be forewarned, though. Every additional question you ask may collect valuable info you can use, but you also reduce the number of people who will respond. The more work fans have to put in (or perceive themselves as putting in), the fewer people will participate.

These downloads can also be given away in exchange for a "like" on a social network. There are numerous sites out there such as Rootmusic offering free widgets that basically unlock the download in exchange for signing up to the page. Do some people sign up, get the download and then withdraw? Yes, but very few. Most people will stick it out because it's somewhat a pain to do otherwise.

Multiple social networks should offer different downloads to encourage signups on each one. Remember, you're still playing a numbers game for your hack. You don't want to seem too outlandish, but without a healthy number of social followers, you won't appear like a hit to either the industry or to potential fans. Grow it every way you can, and that includes encouraging people to vote more than once.

Ask for mobile numbers so you can text them when you're in town. (Remember to reassure them that this is why you want it.) Better yet, do it in concert. When you're at a gig, ask people to text you (on a dummy phone discussed in the mobile chapter, no need for the short code stuff) and you'll text them back with a free download link. Maybe even make it a track from that night's show straight from the mixing board. Then, when you get all those numbers, make sure you tag them to the town you played in. Now, next time you come through there, you have a group of fans to text with a reminder about where you're playing. Or you can hit them up to do other things, such as watching a YouTube video.

Don't hit them up a lot; do it strategically.

The best way is to ask for an action that will promote you. You may already have acquired a fan's email and seen her sign up to your social networks. In that case, give away something in exchange for an action. Promojam is a unique platform that unlocks content after someone has written a tweet promoting you. You don't have to use them, however. You can also just set up a tweet and monitor it. You can set up a search on Twitter to look for your exact phrasing and then send a link to the free download either on Twitter or Facebook.

See how easy this is? That's a lot of valuable stuff you can get that's worth way more than a micropayment. Each effort is important in its own right, but you can do them separately or in combinations. You may want to space them out so you're giving yourself enough time to create a lot of content to give away. You also don't want people to fulfill all of your requested actions right away and then have to monitor everything all at once. Take your time with this one, but never stop building your fan base.

CARRY A SIGNIFIER

How much time did you spend on choosing your primary image on your Facebook or Twitter profile? I know a lot of artists who agonize over these images. These images represent who they are. Everything about them needs to be expressed in a picture not even covering 500 pixels. I understand why the time is spent on these tiny images. Without them, you won't provide the right visuals to cue the potential fan as to what to expect from you and your music.

Every artist agonizes about variations of this for the duration of their career. Countless hours are devoted to minute choices such as press photos, album covers and the like. So much time is spent on tweaking tiny elements of the images to get them exactly right, free of any imperfections. Most important, the image has to *signify* who they are.

But while you spend countless hours in your beginning stages poring over that first photo shoot to decide which picture should represent you, how much time do you spend figuring out how to represent yourself at the coffee shop? Probably not enough.

Remember, as an evangelist you have to spend every moment you can talking up you. You have to live and breathe your music and spread it to everyone possible. That means people you have never met before. A lot of them. So get over that fear of strangers, and get out there and start meeting people.

Carrying something that signifies who you are just makes it that much easier to start up a conversation. It becomes a reason why people will either talk to you or talk about you. You have to set yourself apart from the other 100,000 musicians releasing music every year. If you can't stand out among 100 people in a bar, how will you stand out on the Web?

Life is full of conversation starters, and it's your job to use them to their fullest. Carry around a guitar. Or just the case. Doesn't matter. It's the signifier that's important. I attended the Toronto Film Festival years ago and was in my seat waiting for the film to start. Before the film began, a woman sat down next to me...with a guitar case. Not what one usually expects in a movie theater. Given the unusual setting and the fact that I'm in the music business, I had to ask. That's how I met Susie Love, a neo-folk singer. She had a guitar with her because she had to bolt straight from the movie to a gig. Susie gave me a CD and, since I couldn't make her gig after the movie, told me about another show later that week. Did I alter my plans to check out her music? Of course. Would I have ever known she existed if she hadn't had that guitar case? You decide.

Your signifier could be something small or large. But wherever you go, people should know you're "the musician in the room," even among a group of musicians. They don't call it "star vibe" for nothing. As long as people assume you are "someone", then you *are* someone.

The signifier also motivates people to come up and talk to you, and that's good. People will take deeper ownership of you and what you offer if they come to you on their own accord. So have something that draws them to you. People spend extra money on T-shirts at concerts because they want to signify their association with that artist. If you wear a T-shirt of a band you like, especially an obscure one, you'll increase the likelihood that a like-minded fan will strike up a conversation. If you have another distinctive piece of clothing or accessory that says something, then you increase the chances someone will want to hear what it says.

You might evangelize to the fullest by only wearing your band's shirts. Does that seem self-exploitative? Sure, but you have to go to the distance to get the fans. Besides, after you are in a location a few times and someone always sees you wearing your artist name, eventually they will come up to you and ask what it's about. Curiosity will get the better of them. All the better to potentially get them as a fan.

My brother-in-law does this for his site, BuddyTV. It's his business, something he's invested a ton of time and money in. He can't let it fail. So every chance he gets, he evangelizes. For him, that means he's never without a shirt that has a BuddyTV logo. I don't think he has anything else in his wardrobe. I suspect he had a BuddyTV T-Shirt on underneath his tuxedo at his own wedding. One thing you can say though: he's a believer in his business. You always know who he is in a crowd.

Start on thinking about what your signifier is. It is clearly something different for everyone, but the important thing is to have one. Stick out from the crowd. Strike up those conversations. Get yourself seen in order to get yourself heard.

SELL YOUR MUSIC EVERYPLACE YOU CAN

Walmart has a driving, evangelical desire to have you shop only at Walmart. Sam Walton's evangelical approach to achieve that goal has led this behemoth to become the dominant retailer in the world. While they aren't 100% ubiquitous, and will certainly never get there, they have probably come as close as any one company possibly can.

But do you shop only at Walmart? Of course you don't. Maybe you're even one of those people who dislikes their business practices and refuse to shop there on principle. Maybe you are in a major urban area where going to a Walmart is actually a long drive and you can't get there regularly.

So why would you limit your music download sales to iTunes alone? Or even just iTunes and Amazon? The reality is that music is mostly a spur-of-the-moment purchase. People buy it on a whim because something about the mood strikes them. Many bands tell me that they sell the most music from the merch stand on the road. There's a good reason. The audience, having just heard music and enjoyed themselves, are excited to continue that experience and buy the music on impulse.

That impulse sale is one reason I speak so often. I sell just as many books at speaking engagements as I do on Amazon. The music industry has lost sight of this important sales philosophy, and that has negatively impacted revenues. A decade ago, one could go into any shopping center and find more than one place to buy music. Now, there's almost no place where you can buy music. Those few stores that carry music relegate it to the back, with no promotion in the store window.

Despite its overall popularity, music is no longer treated as a sales draw by stores. This second-class status has largely decimated those impulse purchases that used to drive so much revenue. Dedicated music fans will always be able to find music. But the casual buyers whose life won't change whether they have music or not...they're the ones who make the profitable difference for a hit. Going after music fans will get you a niche, but it won't get you a hit.

This means you have to make sure your music is available for sale anywhere the potential fan has that impulse to buy. If you fail to grab them at that point, most likely they won't buy it at all, and you won't have your hit.

To overcome this, you need to be everywhere you can be. Your strategy: be everywhere you can be. If you sign up for a music distribution service, they will offer you several sites where you can make your music available. Check them all, without hesitation. You need ubiquity, not just locations that fit you perfectly. Heck, check out all the independent digital distributors to see who services music to the most sites. Maybe one site costs more, but gets your music out to more sites to sell. Take it. Getting more copies sold should be a top goal now, before you worry about getting those extra pennies. That can come later after you have your hit.

Once that's taken care of, don't rest. Find and contact other sites that fit your style of music, even if your aggregator doesn't sell to them. A great example is Beatport, which focuses on the electronic music community. Their popularity within their niche is so important that you can't have a dance hit without being on their site. Every genre has such sites. Find and get on all of them.

Then, find other sites that have nothing to do with music, but have everything to do with you as an artist. Here's an example: In the '90s, there was a fun novelty band called the Zambonis. As their name implied, they only sang songs about hockey. In those early Internet days, it was easy for them to reach out to the NHL. They stated the obvious. "We're a band that sings about hockey. You're the top hockey organization. Sell our CDs on your Website." They sold thousands. They also wrote a theme song for the Colorado Avalanche and played it at one of the team's Stanley Cup Final appearances. You never know where reaching out will lead you.

Sure, the big sites may not return your emails or phone calls. That's OK. If you're in a niche, go for the smaller sites that also reach those niches. They could grow into bigger entities. Even if they don't, the important thing is that if someone is thinking about you at the moment they hit that site, they have the opportunity to buy.

Maybe these smaller sites don't have a store. Give them one. Sign up for any of the retail Web services that you may use on your own Website (Topspin, Bandcamp, etc.) and ask your targeted sites to put up a widget selling your music. Maybe they'll embed it underneath an article they write about you. Maybe they'll put it in a "cool stuff" section. Or maybe they'll say no. But you lose nothing by asking.

And did you add those buy links to your Facebook and Twitter profiles? Make those widgets readily identifiable on your social networking site, and you'll increase the likelihood that a visitor to your page will buy your music.

Take nothing for granted. Try to sell through every avenue you can think of. Leave no stone unturned. Every little bit will count on establishing your song as a hit.

IDENTIFY FANBASE BY FANS

Who likes you? That is, besides your mom? At least I <u>hope</u> your mom likes your band. Well, except maybe for that sexually explicit song. I get why she doesn't like that. After all, Mom does want to be proud of you.

So, okay, aside from your family, who likes you? What are their ages? What bands do they like? What clubs do they go to? What sites do they visit? These are all important things in determining who your prospective fans might be.

Some of this intelligence is readily available. Aggregated fan profiles from sales on iTunes and Amazon are good places to go. You should also be collecting a reasonable amount of information from your database. For example, from my Topspin account, I can see where my fans live, and get a good idea of their age and sex. I'll also see how that changes over time, adjusting strategies along with my shifting database.

The more technologically advanced and/or affluent can also scrape research sites to get a profile. Companies like Colligent will go through all of your Facebook fans and aggregate everything about them: their favorite books, TV shows, products, etc. That could lead to sponsorship opportunities, because you can show a relationship between your audience and specific brands. Other companies, such as Crymson Hexagon can examine the tweets of your fans to determine what topics tend to come up most often. Use the data from your YouTube video plays by clicking Insight. Buy some plays on Jango and get a quick profile on who likes your music. Quite frankly, the sky's the limit on finding out what you'd like to know. Google an idea, and the company that can find it for you will likely pop up.

For a few bucks, you can do a one-month subscription to SurveyMonkey and just ask your fans anything and everything you want. Offer a carrot at the end: a free live download, a special Webchat, half-price tickets. It doesn't matter, so long as you make sure there is an offer in the mix. Don't go overboard, but certainly you can get away with getting a dozen questions or so before people get upset that you're asking too much.

If you ask for information, make sure you let your audience what the results are. Put together a blog post with some fun facts about their fellow fans. Mention them in a Facebook post to further engage them. If your fans like a particular TV show, arrange a viewing party online where you watch and comment along with your fans. You can have fun letting them know the results of the survey.

The bottom line is that making the effort is the most important part. Many artists assume they are one thing when, in actuality, they are another. That could be a blow to the ego, but you gotta suck it up if you want that music to be a hit. If you don't, you have to recognize that your music isn't reaching your intended target and that you need to tweak your music to attain your desired audience. But if you keep finding your audience is something else, face facts or face a lack of hits.

Once you zero in on who your fans are, you can do a wealth of things described throughout this book. You can go after those fans and achieve a higher likelihood that they'll enjoy your music. You might even reach out to some of the artists your audience also likes and suggest swapping info. Promoting each other. Touring together. Stranger things have happened.

CRAIGSLIST

Listen to people. I can't stress that enough. Listen to your fans. Listen to your friends. Listen to friends of your friends. Never let your eyes glaze over. You never know when a comment will grow your audience.

This hack came courtesy of just such an encounter. I was in a seedy club in Amsterdam. Beer was cheap, graffiti was everywhere. The building it was in had been taken over by squatters, who ran the joint. Certainly not the place I'd expect to get an idea, much less one that would be a chapter in this book.

The DJ, Chad Jones, was spinning some cool dubstep, and the night was getting into an early groove. After his set, he came over to chat and began to talk about how hard it was to get his music noticed in Amsterdam and to make any money. In fact, the most lucrative thing he had ever gotten was on Craigslist.

Say what?

Turns out that Chad was wandering around Craigslist and found a Christian band in the U.S. looking for someone to remix one of its songs for the electronic market. They didn't have much money, hence trying to find someone cool on Craigslist. He answered the ad, they liked his stuff, he got the gig. One band's low pay is another man's payday.

How many times have you looked on Craigslist looking for work? The thought hadn't even occurred to me until Chad mentioned it. As soon as he did, though, a world of potential hacks opened up for me that could be possible using Craigslist.

Start by giving out free things via Craigslist. Tailor the ad as specifically as you can for maximum impact. Are you going to play a gig in Atlanta? Put up an ad in the Atlanta Craigslist advertising the free MP3, with info on your gig. If one person shows up, that's still one more fan than you had before. And that fan may bring a friend. Advertise "specials." Ask people to print out the ad (with their email address on it) and present it to receive something free at your merch booth.

Organize special events through Craigslist. See if you can get together a jam session while you're in town. Be the catalyst.

On the flip side, answer as many relevant ads as you can. Someone looking to start a band that has a similar profile? Send them a nice message with a free MP3 link saying you thought they might like it.

Can't find a place to play in a certain town? Organize and advertise that you'll do a free show. Maybe there's a coffeehouse looking for talent. See if you can do an acoustic show.

Use it to get to know other musicians in other towns. Maybe someone's looking for a guitar part that you can lay down quickly. Reach out and start a friendship. Swap music. Start growing. Someone selling a guitar usually means they have some musical inclination. It might not make sense to respond to the first 99 guitar ads, but No. 100 could be magical.

Also, be on a constant lookout for similar sites that may have smaller communities, but are still large enough to find fans. Sites like Oodle have the same basic function with a different design. Ebay Classifieds might yield some interesting connections depending on your search. Bandmix allows musicians to post classifieds about themselves to find potential work. They may also like your music if you reach out nicely.

The reality is that Craigslist is full of people who are in the same boat you're in; they just may not be expressing it as well as you can. Banding together is crucial, so help each other, and each one of you can grow. All those relationships become seeds. I'm sure you could wander through Craigslist and find many more ideas. It's a world of unlimited possibilities. Email me your thoughts. Let's get the conversation started!

And best of all, it's free.

IDENTIFY
SUPERFANS

You're playing a show and there's a person in the front row, screaming her head off. She knows every word to every song. She never leaves to get a beer or go to the bathroom. She appears to have a devotion to you that borders on really, really scary. After the show, you meet her and express your gratitude. She promises that she'll be at every show in town and may even drive to a few others. And then...what do *you* do?

That person is a superfan, and if you let her out of your grasp, you're an idiot. Superfans are not just people who know everything about you. They will also be the ones most likely to tell everyone they know about how great you are. They will also be the ones to spend the most money on you. If they are your most passionate customers, how should you treat them?

Let's look at this objectively. You own an independent coffee shop in a town filled with coffee shops. Starbucks and Coffee Beans dot every other block, not to mention the coffee in places like McDonald's, Panera or even gas stations. You've got immense competition, and if your coffee shop is going to remain open, you've got your work cut out for you.

So a customer comes up to you and says, "Wow, this is the best coffee in town! I can't believe the difference. I plan on coming here at least three times a week." What do you do? Of course, you say, "Thank you," to show your appreciation. But then what?

Did you get that customer's information? A simple question could be, "Can I get your email so I can keep you up to date on special offers and events?" Did you give that customer something to spread the word? How about, "Here's a bunch of $1-off coupons for your friends. I hope they'll try us out." Heck, did you even ask their name?

Simple questions? Obvious marketing tricks? Not for everyone. While I was writing this book, a restaurant opened up near my house featuring a specific ethnic food that is hard to find in my area. I expressed excitement to my wife, and we went there for lunch the next day. We were thrilled that the food was delicious, but were worried because we were the only ones eating there. Only one other person came in for take-out while we ate.

Afterwards, I thanked the owner/chef for such a great meal and told her we'd be telling all our friends. I even tweeted about it from that spot. She was very appreciative, but she offered nothing in return other than thanks.

We returned to the restaurant five days later with guests, and again we thanked her. A few days later, we had a party and ordered a couple of catering trays. All said and done, we spent about $250 over three visits in a 10-day period, brought additional future customers, and turned others onto their food at our party.

But in that period, she never once asked my name, nor did she ask me to sign up for any sort of mailing list. She didn't ask if I would hand out cards or coupons to our party guests, which I would gladly have done. She recognizes me when I walk into the restaurant, so she clearly identified me as a superfan of her restaurant, but took no action to bring me in deeper. She is relying on the fact that I will come in on my own volition. I likely will, but what happens when things get busy, and another new place opens up, and more distractions occur? This particular restauranteur is a chef, not a marketer, and perhaps cultural issues affect the way she regards interacting with clientele.

But the power of one person can be significant. Let's assume I spend $250 a month at this restaurant between my family and the guests I bring in. My contribution to the restaurant would be $3,000 in gross revenue a year, not to mention the additional business from the word-of-mouth advertising and repeat visits from guests I entertain there. $3,000 is not too shabby. Using the coffee shop analogy, spending $5 a day over 20 workdays would result in $100 a month, or $1,200 a year. Again, pretty good money from one customer.

Now, can these establishments find and cultivate 100 superfans locally? For an independently owned business, keeping a list of 100 people is easily managed. For the coffee shop, those 100 people represent a whopping $120,000 a year. In the restaurant, it'd be $300,000. For such businesses, that revenue alone probably wouldn't keep the doors open, but it sure would go a long way to ensuring they don't close.

What I've just illustrated is a variation of the "1,000 true fans" theory. Popularized by Wired magazine co-founder Kevin Kelly, the theory goes that if you can get 1,000 passionate fans to spend $100 a year on you, you can gross $100,000 and begin to make a living at music. As outlined above, it's actually much easier to get those fans to spend $100 than it is to find others to spend $10 on you when they don't know who you are. The question is, do you know who those 1,000 people are?

You may not have 1,000 fans at the moment, and that's okay, because nobody starts successfully from day one. As Kelly pointed out, if you can add one superfan a day, you can accumulate 1,000 superfans in three years and reach "quit your day job" territory. However, it's up to you to find these people and bring them in.

Start with that obsessive fan at your concert. Get every bit of information you can about her. Make sure you follow up with a contact after the show. A good tip is to get a regular mailing address and send her a thank-you postcard from the next city. Who gets thank-you notes by mail anymore? Who gets them from an artist? Want a fan for life who will always treasure you when you're famous? How about the one who has a framed handwritten postcard proving "I knew you when"? Spend that $1 on a cheap postcard and stamp. That's nothing if you're on the way to getting $100 a year.

Going one step further, in the "There's an App for that" category, you can send a physical postcard right from your phone. The app Postcard On The Run allows you to take an iPhone photo (you and the fan), put in a personal message, and it gets sent out physically to their mailbox. A very cool memento that takes 2 minutes to put together.

For the ones who don't come to the show, are you finding them online? Did you notice the person who wrote on your wall, commented on a message board, or tweeted about you using language a bit more passionate than most? Zero in on that person and treat him like gold. Most people who take the time to post anything are hot leads for superfans. They made the effort, for crying out loud! And you will respond to them by...ignoring them? I think not! Respond to them, friend them, and continue to talk to them.

Keep a separate list of your superfans or just flag them in your overall fan database – whatever helps you find them easily. Create a list on Facebook called "Superfans." Even better, create a list on Twitter called "Superfans." Then watch as people ask you to put them on that list. How much easier can it be when a fan comes up and explicitly says, "I'm a superfan"? Snag 'em!

I know musicians really don't like it when the music business is compared to traditional businesses like coffee shops and restaurants. The reality is that running your career as you would those businesses is a key success factor. Those businesses identify their prime customers and cater to them. Why wouldn't an artist? It's time for you to start identifying *your* superfans.

NURTURE SUPERFANS

Congratulations. You've organized your initial list of superfans. They're passionate and are like seeds ready to flower to show the world your blossoming garden of fans. *Now* what do you do?

One thing you don't do is ignore them. Plan a regular schedule of communication and stick to it. You can always deliver more, but if you keep at least a minimum schedule, you can always guarantee delivering something to that group. It could be every Monday afternoon, or it could be Thursday morning before that weekend's shows. Just put the date on your calendar and make it a habit.

Having said that, so many people deliver Webisodes every week that they begin to drown each other out. Many times the Webisodes just "go up" unannounced and you have to remember to visit a specific page every day to see it when it's fresh. What about making your Webisodes accessible only to superfans for the first 24 hours? There is no better way to remind these fans how special they are than to give them special attention.

Most weekly Webisodes are inane. How many bands do we need to see joking around backstage? If I have to see one more band goofing off with Devil Dogs at a gas station rest stop, I will die from boredom. Give fans what they truly want, which is direct communication. And the reality is that this can be EASIER to do.

All you need to do is sit in front of a camera. Hit record. Say your piece. Hit stop. If you're delivering content Monday mornings, maybe it's a quick news-type report of what happened that weekend. Mention by name the superfans you met! Always remember to recognize them. Talk about the highlights of the show. Let everyone know other interesting people you met. Tell them the troubles you have. People want to know it all.

If you're delivering content before a show, give people special tasks to do when they get there. Have them shout out specific words to get you to play certain songs in the set. Other people at the venue will ask them, "Why did you yell 'Fish in Cancun' at the singer?" That gives the superfan the opening to tell them more about you, how to reach you online and to reel them in as the next superfan.

Ask superfans for feedback about your new music. It's now old hat for artists to ask fans what songs should be "the single" from a new release. It's simple, and it works. Because your fans are your most passionate supporters, they want to tell you that certain songs are great, and other songs aren't up to your potential. It's OK if they don't like a song: If you engage them by asking why and don't repeat the same mistakes, those fans will stick with you. If you fail to engage them, however, those bad songs (and you will have bad songs) will drive them away.

Get your superfans to spread the word about your music. All artists want their music to "go viral." Great. But unless something is in the top .00001% of best content, it won't happen by itself. You have to ask. The good news is that superfans will rarely say no. Give them a fun task with rewards; hold a free Webchat if 1,000 new people download a song, or post a new song if a show sells out.

The secret is to reward not attainment of the goal, but the effort your superfans make to reach it. Who really knows how many downloads you had off of your Website? Only you! So what if your goal was 1,000 and you only got 238. This is the music business. A bit of hype is part of the game. Did you know that gold and platinum records are based on records "shipped" and not "sold"? If you deliver 500,000 CDs to stores across the U.S., you have a gold record. Doesn't matter if only 20 people buy it. You can still say legitimately that you have a gold record. Now, that's an extreme example of hype, but remember, we're hacking here. It's important to convey the impression of success.

Engagement of superfans is so easy, you'll wonder why you didn't do it before. The key is getting into the routine. It's so hard for many musicians to have a routine; it can seem daunting. But your superfans are waiting. Schedule a set hour every week, and don't let anything get in the way of your time with them.

THE SECOND STAGE OF THE FIRST IMPRESSION

So somehow, word got to me about you. Someone, somewhere, told me that you were good or that your song was good. I want to go check it out. Are you prepared?

In hacking your hit, you've done, it's hoped, a great job in placing your music everywhere. You've made sure your single is easily found. But what about everything else?

When someone is getting a first impression about an artist and/or a song online, there are essentially two stages to that impression. Stage 1A is the method by which someone discovered the artist and/or song. Maybe it was from a blog post, or a friend telling someone about it. Maybe this person picked it up from a friend's Facebook status update. However it happened, something somewhere set someone on the chase to hear the music.

That's when Stage 1B comes into play, when the music and everything surrounding it has to deliver. How this person heard about the music will determine what's needed for that favorable impression. Some blogs have embedded players or download links. In such cases, the songs have to stand on their own merit. Some have embedded video, so you need to make sure the video it links to has all the right visuals.

But many people just surf to their favorite discovery site to search, find, and listen to the song. At this point, everything that surrounds that music is crucial for establishing your hitworthiness. Remember, to hack a hit, you must appear to be hitworthy. (More on this soon.) The experience in getting to your song is equally as important as the song itself.

The tough part is that the ways consumers approach music discovery is ever-changing. Five years ago, it was MySpace, and you had to make sure that your page had all the necessary messaging. Now, there are countless ways for people to hear your music. Fortunately, despite the almost infinite number of websites, there are just a few key experiences that you must get right.

The most notable is YouTube. You did put together your own YouTube channel to house all your official videos and conversations about you, didn't you? If not, get started.

Now, your YouTube channel is merely a tool to aid you in your mission, because people are unlikely to go to your channel during this stage of the first impression. Rather, they are going to a Web page of results based on searching your artist name or song title. What someone sees in this page speaks volumes about who you are, how popular you are and at what level of the game you're at.

The first thing you need to do is to make sure the page is filled with results that relate to you. That means that you have to get videos posted. The first logical place for these is on your channel. That's a great start, but a YouTube search won't list the 20 or so results just from your channel. So you need to add to it from other accounts. Have your friends post videos. Make up several new accounts and post from them. The how is not as important as just getting it done.

Before uploading, pay careful attention to titling and tagging. Make sure you title your videos with "Artist Name" first, followed by "Song Title." Then place whatever other information you'd like. Make sure you place your name and the song title in the tags, too. In short, leave nothing to chance. You need to make sure your content comes up when it gets searched.

Your clips should be diverse. Place the studio version of your song against a simple picture of you. Make another version that has the lyrics scrolling by. Do a live acoustic version in your bedroom. Then, go to the bedroom next to you and have a friend cover the song. Do a shaky phone cam version of the song next time you're performing at a club. That's five versions right there without even digging for ideas. You're on your way. The total cost is the camera and your time.

Now you may start thinking, "OK, I put up all these versions, but if nobody's watched them, would they come up in a search?" The answer is yes. While writing this section, I was listening to a bunch of assorted music that was sitting in my hard drive. This part of the chapter happened to coincide with a song that grabbed my attention called "Counting On Disaster" by Curtis Peoples.

So, here's a case of a relatively unknown song. I searched YouTube for that song title; it contains some rather generic words, so I thought there'd be a good chance I wouldn't find it. But I did. The top nine search results were all for Curtis performing the song at various venues. The astonishing thing was that several of the performances were three years old, and none had more than 117 views. This song certainly qualified as obscure. The search, however, was successful because multiple versions had been uploaded. Had this obscure track been limited to one live performance from years ago, I would assume that nobody much cared for Curtis. Instead, I found that he's been performing for awhile, plays up and down the East Coast and was on a cruise ship concert with Sister Hazel in 2009. A lot of decent information.

The content just needs to be there. The next step, after that, is to get your superfans, friends and family to start watching. You are correct in assuming that having more views creates the impression of popularity. You don't, however, need millions of views. Getting above 10,000 on some key titles is good enough to show that something is going on. Can you get 1,000 fans to watch 10 times each? Not an insurmountable figure. If you're really lazy about it, you can always purchase these plays. Certainly, that's a hack, so it's worth mentioning. Just Google that to find vendor sites, if you're so inclined. The truth, though, is that 10,000 is an achievable number by your own efforts.

The next logical place people will look for you is Google. This one's a little harder, but there is some low-hanging fruit you need to harvest immediately. Start by getting your friends, family and superfans to search for you. "But they already know how to find my music," you say. True, but this is all about impression – which brings us back to our conversation about *first* impressions, specifically Part B, Google's Instant Search. When you dive in, you see suggestions on what you're searching for before you finish typing it. If your term fails to come up, it suggests that you and/or your song is not popular.

Avoid this by asking your close circle to search for these terms early in the game so that even your first potential fans will have no problem finding you. Don't just do "Artist Name," "Song Title" and "Artist Name + Song Title". Look at suggested searches for songs that are similar to yours. Lyrics may pop up often. Video may show up. Jot those ideas down for future reference. You may also need them later on for cheap keyword buys on Facebook or Google.

Google performs so many searches for so many things, it takes just a couple of dozen people searching terms for it to start listing them as suggestions. If you build them correctly, these suggestions will most certainly make a positive impression about the status of your song. Don't wait for popularity to come to you. Create the impression that you're already popular.

Naturally, the results need to be there too. This makes things a bit more difficult, but not impossible. Many lyric sites allow you to post lyrics to any song. Don't wait for a fan to do it; you do it. And do it before you release the song, on all the sites you can. Yes, you'd like people to read the lyrics on your site, but that's less important at the moment. Right now, you want to give the impression that you're popular. Google also weights as its top listings the sites that get a lot of traffic. Sites such as lyricsmania.com probably get way more traffic than you do. True, most potential fans won't click to these sites. The important thing is that the first search results page is filled with stuff about your song.

Where else can you add updates? Wiki sites are everywhere. Wikipedia is the most obvious one (and it has the most traffic), so start there. Just Google "Music Wiki" and see what new sites are popping up. You may not be able to post on all of them, but you can probably find a few to make sure you've got some results showing up.

Get your friends' blogs to post stuff about your song. You don't have to beg for a heavy-duty review. A simple photo and link to your Facebook or YouTube profiles will suffice. Just make sure they type out your artist name and song title in the headline and the body of the blog, with other key words like "music." No friends? Make your own blog. Just be sure you also put a couple of other stories up there on other artists, so the site has the appearance of appealing to a wide audience.

Make sure you've got your artist profiles on as many sites as you possibly can. Hit all the big ones, such as Reverbnation, last.fm and Purevolume. And make sure you're putting your key songs in all of these places, as they need to come upon the search results, too.

The beauty about search results is that the more you're out there, the more your search results improve overall. Ideally, you want places that link to your site, but you'll get there. Right now, nobody knows you or your song. So you need to get out the word that you and your music exist in as many places as you can. At this stage, no nook or cranny is too small. They're tiny building blocks that form the foundation for success.

Remember, you are conveying the impression that you are *happening*, that there are many places on the Web talking about you. If people search for you and see only one or two results, however good they may be, the impression is that you're not popular. Don't think of this as pulling the wool over the eyes of a potential fan. If you're worried about that, you're in the wrong business. And you have no reason to worry, anyway. You're just posting lyrics and links to your songs. It's not as if you're claiming you played in front of 20,000 people when it was actually 20. (That happened to me in college when a label rep to our radio station made that claim and thought I wouldn't check up on it!) This is a promotion-oriented business, and you have to create an aura, some mystique and especially buzz around your music. These tools are free and readily available. They're also not used by most artists, so you'll have a head start.

APPEAR TO BE HITWORTHY

There are many clichés out there that revolve around a similar theme: You are how you act. For example, " Perception is reality." "You are as successful as your circle of friends." "How you look is a reflection of who you are" "You are what you eat."

For the next hack, let me give you another one. I'm not even going to claim it as thoroughly original, but it does speak volumes of truth: To have a hit, act as if it already is.

Indeed, one of the underpinnings of this book is that the music business is built on illusion. Record companies spend countless hours and a lot of dollars trying to convince the world that a particular artist is massively huge. When record company promotion people approach me about a new act, more often than not they say a variation of the same line: "This act is gonna be big." By my own unofficial estimate, I'd say they're right about 10% of the time. With those stats, if they played baseball, they'd be kicked off the AAA minor league team. But in the music business, they'd become senior vice presidents.

OK, I kid a bit, but it's true that a .100 batting average meant large-scale success. The end result of this promotional process is that the music consumer has been trained to expect and want a larger-than-life aura around their favorite stars. The issue the modern music business faces today is that the 10% who do have success no longer deliver astronomical results. They just deliver merely great numbers. Music business pessimists would say, "Man, that act would've made us $100 million 10 years ago, and now we're only making $20 million." Meanwhile, the music business optimist that I am would say, "Man, stars like that can make $20 million." It's all in how you look at it.

But despite the decline of music sales, the hype has persisted. This is true not only because record labels practice it, but also because the audience still demands it.

Time and again, artists who project that they are more famous than those listening to the music achieve more success. This does not mean those artists act arrogantly, although that has worked on rare occasion. It just means that everywhere the music fan looks, they see signposts that suggest stardom.

Extreme examples of this phenomenon are gossip magazines and sites like Us Weekly and TMZ. These businesses have actually grown in recent years, reflecting the audience's desire to observe stardom. But the world has flattened, and we're now in a world where we've outgrown our local circle of 40-50 friends. Now we have profiles of hundreds or thousands of friends on social networks, including some of the very celebrities we're discussing. As it's become easier to befriend someone, the desire for a class that's above the average person increases. Your fans want you to be more important than they are.

Of course, this provides a very interesting conundrum. How are you supposed to be super-famous and yet accessible to these same people? Good question, and one not easily answered. Achieving that balance is what separates great artists from the merely good ones. It's a fine, imperfect line that you just need to walk. Don't worry about getting it exactly right. Just work on integrating some of these ideas, as you deem appropriate.

Here's an example: Don't respond to emails right away. I don't care if you only get two a day. The fan doesn't know if it's two, 200 or 200,000. Fans aren't stupid, but they do assume you get way more than you actually do. Don't give them reason to believe otherwise. If you take awhile to respond (we're talking 12 hours to two days, not weeks), then the perception is that you're busy, with a lot of fans to attend to. This works in two ways. It gives the impression that you're busy, and it makes the fan likely to respond immediately.

I bring this up because there are two schools of thought on how you should respond to people in business. In this era of instant communication, many say that a solid business should respond within minutes. This can work when you've got an e-commerce business with millions of dollars in orders and a large customer service department. The flipside here is that a quick response suggests that you will send a quick response to anything. Before you know it, you've got fans emailing you at 6 AM every day asking, "Hey there! How was your night?" Do you need to be answering that all the time? Stars don't, I can tell you that much.

On the other side, though, don't let too much time go by. A marketing company, Hornstein Associates, did a survey in 2007 asking companies for their response time to customer service requests. Nearly half of those surveyed never even answered. Waiting longer than, say, a week really shows your fans that you don't care a lot about them. If you've become a big star (world tours, sales plaques), then fans don't expect a response. But until that point, they do. Imagine walking into a store, wandering around and hoping someone who works there will come up and help you, but no one does. That's the feeling fans get when there's no response.

So you have to set the boundaries with your fans, and for the most part, they must be subtle. Maintaining a slight delay in responding helps you communicate stardom while still retaining fans. Just be certain to set up some time each day, to ensure fans hear from you. By the way, the time of day you respond also speaks volumes. Sending emails at 4pm suggests that, while the rest of the world is working, you've got nothing to do. The ideal time to email is late at night. This works because fans will assume that you've had a big, long day writing, recording and playing, but even though you're tired or might rather be partying, you'd prefer to get back to fans. It also works because your fans are more likely to be asleep, which means they are unable to reply immediately.

The content of your response is also an indication of how much a star you are. If someone says to you, "I really love your new song and I hope it becomes a big hit for you," how would you respond? A natural response might be, "Thank you, and I agree with you. I hope this one's a big smash." However, all you're doing there is reaffirming that the song is not a hit. While you can't lie and claim it's No. 1 on the iTunes chart, you can embellish a lot. A better way might be, "Thank you! So many people have been telling me this since the track came out that I'm still in disbelief. This is my fastest-growing hit ever, so keep telling everyone about it!" Taking a minute to put together a thoughtful response can communicate so much. Remember, you are creating the impression of a hit. It would be unlikely that any of the above would be a false statement about your song. Embellishing? Sure, but you're hacking here. Make yourself big.

When you're writing your blog entries and social network updates, think about all you can communicate that makes you seem bigger than you actually are. Embellish everything that you can. Round up on every stat that makes sense. Don't just say, "Much love to musicsite.com for linking to us!" when you can say, "My Facebook requests have been out of control all day ever since musicsite.com wrote that piece proclaiming how great we are!" I can assert that my first book, Futurehit.DNA, was a #1 Music Songwriting Book on Amazon.com. Is it there today? Probably not. Amazon updates their charts hourly. So I only needed one hour at the top to own this stat. And how many music songwriting books are sold daily, anyway? Who cares! In the world of songwriting books, mine was at the top. That's all I needed to be able to promote something that sounds significant.

Can you find stats that emphasize similar things for you? Are there credible sites, such as Amazon or ReverbNation, where you can direct some energy to your fans in a short burst to obtain the chart position you need? Maybe you can group several credible sites into a useable statistic. I know one artist who has won a dozen prizes in songwriting competitions. Few know that only one of those competitions is really of any importance. Another artist can honestly proclaim that they perform more than 200 shows a year. Never mind that at least 50 of them are last-minute pick-up gigs at 11 on Monday night in front of two people, or that they sometimes performed short sets at two different clubs in the same night. But saying that you play more than 200 shows a year makes you appear to be an artist in demand, as well as a hard worker. Most artists can find SOME venue to book them at the last minute in a bad slot for no money or tips. Find your stats and make yourself more hitworthy.

Getting fan comments online is another very effective hack for making an impression. A lot of people utilize this to suggest popularity, and with good reason. The typical music fan with too little time on his hands will see something on iTunes and YouTube with a ton of comments, look at the topline number and then make a popularity judgment. Frankly, at this point, what the comments say isn't as important as the quantity of them. Of course, you want many positive comments and you should push fans to help get you there. That overall stat, though, speaks volumes.

Similarly, the "like" button that started on Facebook has now spread to many sites. Seeing a large topline number of "likes" on several sites is crucial to moving the needle on people's impression of your popularity. As with YouTube views, these "likes" are important enough that there are companies you can hire to buy them for you. I'm not for that, but it is a consideration. Of course, a huge number of "likes" doesn't guarantee that you will be successful. At your early career stage, it's about growing the *impression* of a hit. The number of comments doesn't prove much of anything in itself. But you're assembling the puzzle pieces that persuade potential fans to find you hitworthy. People make snap judgments, and the number impression is one of the snappiest.

Another influence on snap judgments about your hitworthiness is the number of Twitter followers you have. In another chapter, I discuss how to hack your way to attracting more Twitter followers. A key component of hitworthiness, however, is to make sure that the number of people following you exceeds the number you follow. While it's a good technique to pick up followers in hopes they'll follow you, always be wary of the balance. Constantly cull the people you follow to make sure that this ratio stays at a respectable number. You don't need to have a 100:1 ratio, but at your stage a 5:1 ratio or greater is a good goal to work towards.

　　　Again, it's all about impressions. The music fan still can succumb to hype. You might even correctly surmise that with all the distractions consumers experience every day, they actually *need* the hype to filter what they are supposed to listen to. Record companies are constantly hacking when to create hype in order to make an artist successful. There's no reason you shouldn't do the same. While the dollars needed for widespread radio play and publicists to get you into major gossip publications may be out of your reach, there are enough smaller things you can hack for free that can start a hitworthy aura. At this point, you're not looking to compete with Lady Gaga. You're looking to convey the impression that there's enough activity to give you the *potential* to be the next Lady Gaga. And that, my friend, is something you can start doing today.

PRETTY GIRLS

OK, this one may seem obvious. It's also not for everyone. I also feel a little bit uncomfortable even mentioning it. However, if I'm going to give you every tip I know on how to get your songs noticed and become more hitworthy, I have to mention it. I also have to mention it in a slightly crude way that former team members of mine came up with, just because it's the best way to remember it.

Hot chicks get clicks.

There's a reason that major labels like casting scantily clad women in music videos. It works. There's a reason that you're more likely to see a female image on front pages of major Internet portals like Yahoo! and Huffington Post. It works. There's a reason Spinal Tap's *Smell The Glove* album flopped. They failed to put a woman on the cover.

I don't really need to explain it to you, do I?

If you're a female artist, don't feel afraid to make yourself as attractive as possible. That's what your competition is doing. Also, if you're trying to appear hitworthy, then looking attractive is part of that aura. Embrace it.

If you're a male artist, having attractive women in your videos keeps viewers engaged. You may also want these women in the front row of your live videos. I once went to a show by an aging classic rock artist that was being taped for broadcast. They hired models to dance at the edge of the stage. They didn't want the artist's true fans (grey-haired fat guys) to be up front. These women can pose with you, appear in your still photos or interview you in a fan video. Whatever makes sense.

Where you put these images of attractive females is even more important than having them in the first place. When you place a video on a site like YouTube, you have a thumbnail image. Use this to draw the click-through to your music. Make sure the most attractive image with a female is included. When you're making a YouTube video that's just still images and you want to include a live shot indicating how great you are in concert, what type of shot do you include? A shot of your band giving all members "equal time?" Or a shot of the lead singer leaning off the stage to a throng of hot women with their arms outstretched?

When you highlight shots of you and your fans, are you highlighting the overweight music geek or the pack of college girls? When you retweet fan photos, do you use generic shots of the band in action, or are you emphasizing the young females? When you make a video, how many females are in the video? How often do you go to shots of them?

If you still believe that your music will carry you to the finish line of success, I can't and won't try to dissuade you from that notion. However, don't say I didn't warn you about a reality that has been an important element for most bands ever since the advent of video. It's not for everyone or every situation. And it's definitely not something to overuse. However, it *is* something to be cognizant of.

GOOGLE SEARCH BAND NAME

You and your band mates got together. You wrote down a bunch of ideas and decided that the best name for your hair metal throwback band is Satan's Spawn. Everyone nodded in agreement, and the bassist got to work on the ultra-cool logo. Several months later, the band is playing out, releasing some music and getting the t-shirts printed. There's only one problem.

You never Googled the band name.

Why should anyone bother to do this? Shouldn't the unique creativity of the band brainstorm be enough? In an idealized world of the past, maybe. But today, this step is crucial to having the opportunity to make a hit. Let me explain.

First, simply check if there's another band with the same name. In the "old" days, you relied on your knowledge of existing bands, which essentially consisted of two types of artists – a successful one or a local one. If a band had been on a record label and recorded a few hits or more, it was obvious someone had claimed that name. No sense calling your band the Eagles, for example. It was also pretty easy to determine local band names. If the band Satan's Spawn showed up in a local club listing, you chose an alternate band name.

The only way to ensure that your group's name did not duplicate another's was to do an expensive trademark search, which involved hiring a lawyer. However, are lawyers and the companies they hire to do this really adept at discovering semi-obscure metal bands around the world? Some are, some aren't.

As a result, bands often had to change their name. Sometimes worldwide, sometimes locally. In the early '90s, a band out of England called Suede exploded onto the scene with a mountain of hype. They quickly crossed the Atlantic and started creating noise in the US. There was only one problem. A lounge singer popular in the gay community also recorded by the name Suede and had been doing so for several years. Litigation ended with the band changing its name to "The London Suede," which caused a lot of confusion. Back when there were record stores, it wasn't clear whether they were filed in the "S" or "L" section? Casual fans might have wondered whether it was the same band. The new name also was decidedly clunky.

When a band needs to change its name, it is changing its branding. That's a risk, because branding is absolutely key in retaining a fan base. After making a change, the super-passionate fans might stay with you. However, most fans just don't pay that much attention. In a very A.D.D. world, you can't risk any changes that may cause your potential fan not to engage with your music.

Bottom line: You want to avoid ever changing your artist name, at all cost.

Take two minutes and Google your name right now. What do you get? You can learn instantly if there's another band anywhere else in the world that has laid claim to the same name. You can see where they're from and what level of popularity they might have. That quick search can save you a lot of heartache later on. You'd be surprised how many artists still fail to do this and commit themselves to a name that's already been taken.

While you're at it, also try subtle variations of your name. Slight name changes, tiny misspellings, anything you can think of. Spend those extra few minutes. You never know what you might come up with. You might well find results that guide you to make a name change to avoid confusion.

For example, at the SXSW conference in Austin in 2011, I was hanging with some music industry friends. The group recommendation was to see a new Nashville-area band called Those Darlins. Coincidentally, I had run into two members of this group a few weeks earlier, so I was interested in checking the band out. We went into the club, waited for the band to set up, and they began to play. There was just one problem: The band playing included members who were clearly not the artists I had met two weeks earlier.

I looked through my notes and realized my mistake. The band I had met was The Darlins, not Those Darlins. Both were from Nashville, but were, of course, entirely different groups. Now, I'm in this business and am supposed to detect differences like this. But the average music fan is not. If you recommend "Those Darlins" to your friend, and they then go online and find "The Darlins" and decide they don't like it, how long will it take for the artists to realize the confusion? Unless they get a No. 1 record, they probably never will.

Don't be so precious about how you think of your name. Think of how people will speak it. In the above examples, they may be cute about using "Darlins" but you have to assume that people will also search "Darlings" and may struggle finding you. The artist Ke$ha had some rough goings in her early days. For one, it's tough to search for a dollar sign. For another, most people thought her name was pronounced KEE-sha or kay-SHA. They searched for those spelling variations and largely came up empty. This slowed down her ascent to fame, though certainly it didn't hamper her long-term success.

A name that is easily understood verbally took a giant leap forward in October 2011 when Apple introduced Siri as part of the iPhone. The app helps you find information by simply speaking the question or statement into the phone. This works well for weather, directions and calendar info, but it routinely gets tripped up around band names. A search for the group Hotels And Highways turned up information on local hotels. When I asked the question, "When is Kesha playing in concert?" I got a list of local movie theatres.

So, yes, you want to avoid this confusion at all costs. Because music is entertainment, it is your job to make music discovery easy. Don't make it hard for potential fans to find you. If something obvious like this pops up, make the change before it's too late.

Confusion around bands is easy to identify. How about confusion around everything else in the world? Whether you like it or not, you are up against everything else that shares the same name you have chosen for your band. So before you commit, you must identify who shares your space and how easy it will be for you to be found in that space.

The good news is that music by nature tends to be highly indexed, and so are sites that feature music and music-related content. This is everything from YouTube and iTunes to Amazon and Wikipedia. Once you place your music within these services, your name begins to have a decent advantage over other forms of content that can serve you well.

The bad news is that other names may be so big that you'll just have a very tough chance of breaking through. In 2010, I criticized the success of an artist named Sam Adams. He literally came out of nowhere to have a No. 1 selling rap album. I, and several other bloggers, was skeptical that the sales were legitimate. One sign was the lack of presence on the search term "Sam Adams." Despite the sales success, nothing related to him as an artist could be found. If he had sold his record at under-the-radar record stores, this might have been easily explained. Since the records were all sold digitally, the lack of presence on search was a huge red flag.

In fact, the rapper was legit, and he had a modest hit. But it was unsustained, partially owing to this lack of search presence. His competition was fierce. He had to compete with both an historical figure and a beverage. In search results, there can be only one, and it would take a much greater degree of popularity to be highly listed. This meant people would have difficulties in finding links to his music.

It also put him in a detrimental position from a psychological perspective. The inability to have a top search result conveys the impression that you haven't made it. If you aren't at "the top," then you're not a hit. If he were truly that popular, he would be found more easily. Had Sam Adams chosen a unique moniker, there likely would not have been questions surrounding his chart debut.

You might ask, "But, Jay, Sam Adams is his name." True, but if your name causes confusion, you still have a problem. You wouldn't name your act Billy Joel, right? (Actually, you can't, because Billy copyrighted his name.) You'd want to avoid any conflict with him. Never compete with any name that may be too popular to overcome.

If you're using your real name, it's highly unlikely that it's unique. So certainly, when you search your own name online, you are almost certain to find a result for someone else. The question is whether that person is more popular than you have the potential to be with just a little effort.

Some situations are obvious. If you have the same name as a dentist in Sheboygan, you're probably safe. If it's a state representative, you might think about it. However, you're still probably safe, as state politicos don't normally attract a lot of inbound links to push up search results.

What happens when your name is shared with a second-tier sports figure? You may never watch NASCAR or European football, and therefore have no idea who their stars are. These sports regularly attract crowds larger than nearly every top music star can draw in concert. You definitely don't want to compete against those fans. If that happens, you become invisible very quickly.

What happens if you share the name of a person who committed a heinous crime? It may not. Notorious figures in the public eye at any level, however, can be very hard to compete against with search terms. Even if the crime is relatively low profile, would you be comfortable knowing people looking for you will possibly relate to you in this negative fashion? (Well, maybe if you're the singer of Satan's Spawn!)

It's understandable that you may be reluctant to change your name if it's the one you were born with. However, this is a controllable element, and anything you can control to gain a competitive advantage is worth pursuing. I will personally apologize to your parents for needing to adopt a stage name, but it's probably for your own good. Don't forget that the top-selling digital artist as of 2011 is not Stefani Germanotta.

With music being so fiercely competitive, you have to adapt everything around your music to stand out in the best possible way. Some things, like genre styles, may be unavoidable. However, many choices you make around your music are within your control. When you have the option to create a situation that makes you easier to find, you must take it. Failing to do so is equivalent to resigning yourself to "hope for the best." This thought process starts at the top, with your name. If your own identity is difficult to find, imagine how hard it will be for others to find out everything else about you. Speaking of which...

GOOGLE SEARCH SONG NAME

I love the song "Let's Dance." It's a fun, up-tempo number. Really gets me tapping and humming along. I have great memories from a cassette I owned which had that song on it. Just mentioning the name of the song puts a smile on my face. I love the song, even though I don't know any other song that singer has done.

Wait, are you questioning me and my musical knowledge? How I, as someone who needs to have an encyclopedic brain for this stuff, couldn't recall any other song this artist done? Well, his career was so long ago that it just passed me by.

You say this artist had a very long and legendary career? No, he didn't. "Let's Dance" was his only hit. Are you sure this guy has made numerous albums over many decades? I could've sworn he only had a brief career in the early '60s.

Naturally, I'm talking about Chris Montez. Who were you thinking of?

Of course, the confusion over song titles is far more common than just the above example. There are millions of songs that have been written and released in just the last decade. Are there really that many unique song titles? Well, there certainly are, but the chance that your song title is unique is slimmer than in years past.

In 1983, David Bowie didn't have to worry that a song from 20 years earlier had the same title. One could promote it heavily to radio, and people knew which song was being discussed. The older song was mostly long gone from retail record bins, so there was no confusion of accidentally purchasing the older song with the same name.

The world couldn't be more different today. Most people hear about a song that may be of interest in a social conversation. That could be from people talking to each other, or it could be direct digital messages like text, email or Facebook. However, many discoveries are happening by tracking down the name of the song discussed, not by passing along a link.

The presumption is certainly one that you can just pass along the link, making discovery easy. That's true, but given the level of search volume on song titles, there are many more people who rely on finding the music than there are who expect the music to find them. Perhaps someone did get the link last week, but lost it and now has to track it down. Maybe he forgot to embed the link. Or he just saw the song name in a text message and had to transcribe it into a search box.

Ultimately, the "why" doesn't matter. Just knowing how the discovery process occurs should be enough for you to understand that you must be easy to find. For an artist starting out, it is highly unlikely that the potential listener will associate an artist with a song. Because this is entertainment, most people are just not paying enough attention to get both an artist and song name and then search for both. If an artist is not yet firmly established, but the song has hooks galore, it is more likely that people will remember the song name, not the artist name. So don't count on them searching "song title" + "Artist Name." You can't afford to give the discoverer too much credit.

Make it easy for potential fans and Google not only <u>who</u> you are up against, but also <u>what</u>. In this case, the competition is not just other songs, but other forms of media. Film names often overlap with potential song titles, which makes sense. Both need to be simple, direct and engaging to catch your attention quickly. It gets trickier if the film has had different releases under the same title, or if it's a film that's been remade two or three times. And of course, this situation is not limited to movies. Books are competing for the same frame of reference. For example, before you write that great romantic song, think of how many books Harlequin has churned out over the years, and double-check to see if any of them have already used your title. Kenny Chesney was a big enough star that he could have a song called "You Had Me At Hello" without risking confusion with the film *Jerry Maguire*. But that's an exception.

Now, just because a title has been used before doesn't mean it can't be used again, unless you wanted to name your song "Star Wars." Unlike celebrity names, songs titles tend to be a bit more diffused and therefore have a much looser grip on the upper reaches of a Google search.

People enjoy stories, but they are fanatical about the artists behind them. So when you are weighing possible song titles, be thoughtful about it. Take the time to analyze what search results come up.

If a top result is a Wikipedia entry for another song or movie, stay away. Even though you may never have heard of the song, movie or book, if someone took the time to create an entry, however short, it has some level of popularity or recognition. Even if you believe that the song isn't popular, Wikipedia is. Your song can't effectively compete against that result. You can always try, but this book is about hacking your hit, not how to spend time breaking down a brick wall with a ball peen hammer.

If a top result is coming from a site you've never heard of, there's a good chance that the title has not been used frequently, and yours may be easily found. If you click through on that top link and find a site with poor design and/or a bunch of pop-up ads, even better. These are good indications that your song will be readily found shortly after you release it.

You also need to pay close attention to the video search results. As YouTube increasingly becomes a go-to place for music discovery, many people are going directly to this portion of the results page to find the songs they are looking to listen to. If the title of your song doesn't have any video results showing up, you are certainly in good shape. If the video results have very few views, then you are also likely going to be OK. The trick here is to not ignore these results just because you looked at the text links. These video listings are just as important.

So what do you do if you find that your masterpiece song has a name that is going to be tough to compete against? After all, you shouldn't be forced to change the chorus just because those words might be hard to search for. Instead, look for small, subtler shifts in titling that would improve its optimization for search engines.

The first place I saw this executed to great effect was with Jaron Lowenstein and his group Jaron And The Long Road To Love. In late 2009, he released a new song that was catchy and really grabbed your attention. I called him and said, "Congratulations on your new song. I think "I Pray For You" is going to be a big hit." He responded, "Thanks, but the song is called 'Pray For You.'" Even though you listen to the song and hear "I Pray For You," he lopped off the "I" because that was a title already heavily used. However, he had "Pray For You" all to himself. Is that the perfect solution? Probably not, but when it was written about on blogs, the title stuck and people did catch that subtlety as they searched for the song.

Other times, you just might be the first one to get to a generic term that just doesn't have songs related to it. That may have aided the band Local Natives with their song "Airplanes." While there had been a couple of other songs called "Airplanes" prior to theirs, none of them had been a single. When a few months later, B.o.B released his single called "Airplanes," one would expect some confusion. Instead, in the interest of showing diversified links on search results, YouTube ended up showing them both. In the end, it probably drove some unexpected new fans to the original video. The song received 500,000 views in just six months. The term "airplanes" was also driving 11% of the views to the video.

I've had people challenge me because of the novelty song "Friday" by Rebecca Black. There probably couldn't be a more generic title for a song, and yet it was streamed nearly 100 million times in its first month. That certainly meant it was easy to find. They took this as a sign that you don't really have to worry about making your song title unique.

While this may be true, it also assumes this book was called, *How To Have A Hit By Sheer Dumb Luck.* You can't rely on the Web picking up on you and making you a sensation as a strategy. If you are to hack your hit, you need to strategically plot every nuance to give your music the competitive edge. "Friday" got lucky. If you think your song can overcome those odds, then I also recommend getting your artist financing from the Powerball lottery ticket you plan to purchase.

There are times, though, when you can use popular titles to your advantage. While you may not get the top search result against a popularly used term, you might be different enough to pop up in the Top 10 results. The term may have no video results and so your YouTube video may show up there. Perhaps the term is seldom written about these days because the title is not in vogue. Therefore, a blog entry or news release might show up at the top of those search results. In late 2011, the Foo Fighters had a hit song called "Walk", about as generic as they come. While general search results did not show the song, the video search results did.

When you do this, your song may be able to draft off the familiarity of the term. This is a little risky, because the term does have existing search results. You should evaluate the term beforehand to take a stab at how likely you might be able to be part of the result. Is the term very current? Is its usage very popular among persons and events of big-league stature? Or is it something seldom used? Are the sites among the top A-list results or are they mostly B-list?

It would be reasonable for you to shrug your shoulders and ignore this advice. After all, you wrote the song the way you wanted to. Your creative energy just came out in a particular way, and the song title coincidentally was a widely used phrase. What can you do about it? Plenty. Unless you have a major label bankrolling you, it's extremely tough to compete. Because you're reading this book, I'm assuming you don't have that big wad of money. So do yourself a favor and figure out how to tweak that song. Don't worry if you force a new name or shift a word. You should to at least consider it.

There isn't a perfect way to approach this hack. Dovetailing off of a term could work to your advantage or disadvantage. The key takeaway, though, is to just think about it before you commit. Knowing your competition is half the battle towards success. If you can be aware of it and work with the situation, you just might win big.

HAVE A GIMMICK

I could have called this book *Free And Cheap Marketing Tips For Musicians*. The word "free" always grabs attention. A lot of books have the terms "Free" and "Top" in their titles because authors know they help sell books. Instead, I went with *Hack Your Hit*.

In other words, I had a gimmick. In fact, I had a gimmick even before starting the book. Many authors would bristle at such a notion. After all, shouldn't the focus of an informational, how-to book like this be first about the content, then the marketing? Of course. If I didn't have the content, I wouldn't write the book. On the other hand, if I didn't have the gimmick, I doubt that my otherwise dry title would have enticed you.

As you've probably ascertained from reading this far, the title informed the very tone of the book. Had a straightforward title been used, the book might have been a dry tome. It would have had the same information, but do you think it would have had the same protagonist's voice suggesting, in many ways, how to exploit or counteract the system? Would the details be as well retained if they were presented clinically? The answer is probably not.

I have no interest in writing a conventional book. My first book, *Futurehit.DNA*, presented many challenges, primary among them finding a way to make dry, analytical information into an engaging read for musicians. I just don't have it in me to write scholarly text. My teachers in high school hated that. A little side note about me: When I had to take English tests asking me to write a sentence around each term of grammar, I would actually create a Siskel & Ebert movie review narrative for each one. True story.

So maybe my gimmicks in high school inspired my use of gimmicks in books. After reading *Hacking Work*, the title for this book came to me, and within 10 minutes the framework became clear to me. The most important thing to remember is that the gimmick provides clarity, which, in turn, both informs and sells.

Not only were you likely influenced by the gimmick in your purchasing decision (you *did* purchase this, right?), you are also more likely to tell someone about it as a result. I can't imagine you would be at a club hanging with another act on the bill and say, "Hey, you should read *Free And Cheap Marketing Tips For Musicians*. That book has some good ideas you might use." Instead, it's much easier not only to remember the title, but also to talk about it in a more interesting fashion, such as, "Man, you gotta read *Hack Your Hit*! There's a ton of great secrets on how to become famous."

By the way, if you commit that phrase to memory for those moments, I'd greatly appreciate it. Better yet, memorize it and use it as a secret handshake for other musicians. That way, if you meet them and they finish the phrase, you can both know you're cool hackers. If they don't, I'll leave it up to you to initiate them into the club. Even better: Let me "see" that secret handshake. If you post that phrase on your Twitter account, I'll send you a secret link to download a free bonus hack chapter not included in this book. Yes, buried in the middle of this book, you just found an extra treat. Those people who only skimmed the chapters won't get this additional hack.

Yes, I threw another gimmick into the middle of the chapter on gimmicks. Here's why this is so effective: Hacks such as gimmicks not only inform and sell, they also can form connections. That offer I made enables me to engage in a conversation with you that might not otherwise have been possible. I can then reward you, the reader, for spending time with my writing, which will, I hope, lead you to read my next book. There's also a chance that you'll say to another musician, "That book even has a cool extra thing in it, but you'll only find it if you read it."

Now, replace "reader" with "fan" and start thinking along the same lines for your fanbase. Then you can visualize the value of a good gimmick and start thinking about gimmicks that get people to pay attention to you. My favorite example of that is the band that called themselves

"Free Beer." But also think about ways to *retain* your fans. If you are able to consistently maintain their attention both inside and outside of your music, you'll have a fan for life.

The cool part about this is that the fans want it! Once someone transitions from being a person whose life has been unfulfilled to hearing your music and becoming a richer person for it, they want to play along. It doesn't matter whether you're a sunshine pop artist doing something corny and goofy or a dark gloomy artist exploring your inner blackness. It's all a variation on this theme, so embrace it and have fun with it.

The hardest part of finding a gimmick – when you need to be the loudest – is at the moment when nobody knows who you are. It's easier to take an existing congregation of your fans and give them something fun to do. It's a lot harder to a movement amidst all the musical chatter in the world. It's not easy to execute an idea for breaking into someone's social circle that requires both their attention and time. However, most artists feel that they are above this and don't even try. That's good, because when your competition is the 100,000+ artists releasing music every year, their lack of gimmickry allows you to better compete. Take advantage of it.

And for those of you who still think the idea of gimmicks are corny, let me clue you in. I can probably point out a gimmick that you're already doing, whether you're conscious of it or not. The key difference is whether you embrace it as such and exploit it to its fullest potential to grow your audience.

And don't think using gimmicks makes you phony or superficial. The Beatles wore matching suits and moptop haircuts. For their latest tour, Rascal Flatts wore an all-white wardrobe, while Johnny Cash always wore black. Bono fights for world causes. Willie Nelson supports farmers. Gimmicks appear in numerous forms.

Artists constantly ask me to listen to their music. Managers and artists bombard me with links and bios, all hoping others and I will give their artist a listen. It comes through email, Facebook messages, texts and tweets every day. I do my best to listen to as much as I can. Sometimes, it's in a marathon listening session, which means a band may not get my complete attention just because of where it falls in that session.

That's one reason I'm a sucker for a really good gimmick. And despite what other music purists may tell you, they are as well. Guess what? You probably are, too. Think about where you were when you found out about Rebecca Black's "Friday" video. Now, think about how quickly you went to discover the "world's worst pop song," ahead of other songs of arguably more substance. You succumbed to a gimmick, my friend.

Here's another example: One day I received a tweet from @superstarinsix, the moniker for a NY artist named Jared Weiss. He decided in October 2010 that he was sick of being a struggling artist. So Jared set a goal of having a song in the iTunes Top 10 within six months and created Twitter and Tumblr accounts chronicling his efforts to get there. Even the song he was attempting to do this with, "Bitches All Love Me For My Money," has a gimmicky, attention-grabbing title. While he failed to get into the iTunes Top 10 in the allotted time, he did succeed at one very important thing: He got me to listen. Immediately. And I remembered it.

What you or I think of the song isn't the point, of course; it's the idea of what happened. Jared didn't sell enough by his goal date, but his gimmick attracted the attention of one person (me), who responded to it enough to cite it as an example in a book likely to be read by numerous artists and music business people. That alone helps make him more famous than the frustrated unknown he had previously been. In that spirit, the original impetus for his goal was actually realized.

Check out Jared at www.superstarinsix.com. Then go make your own gimmick.

GOOGLE ALERTS
OF YOU
AND YOUR
COMPETITION

You do use Google Alerts, don't you?

We can talk about how the Internet harmed the music business, but do you know whom it truly decimated? News-clipping services. A decade ago, if you wanted to collect all of the articles written about your band, you hired a clipping service. Most were so expensive that only major-label bands or celebrities could afford them. Today, that "clipping" service is not only more comprehensive, it's also free, thanks to Google Alerts.

It's about as easy to set up as you can imagine. Go to www.google.com/alerts. Type in your search term and how often you want to receive the information. Then the emails start coming. Blogs, news sites, websites, fan sites, social network sites – anytime anyone talks about you (or references anything close to you), it will show up.

In general, this hack is one that most artists I've met have been savvy enough to use, some for several years. After all, it streamlines a process all musicians want and need. The question, however, is how many artists use this tool to its fullest capability.

Let's start with your artist name. Did you set up an alert for your song title? I have alerts for both my name and my book's name. Interestingly, they seldom yield the same results. The title alert often gives me information that the name alert doesn't catch. Maybe someone was discussing the book, but they couldn't remember my name. Maybe they just didn't bother to put my name down. Either way, if I expected to get everything by my name only, I'd miss those results.

When you get a result from sources who knew your song but not you, reach out to them. If they wrote about you, there's a good chance they are fans. Best to do what you can to turn them on to the rest of your music. Motivated by nothing more than a nicely worded thank you note, many of these people will do a lot to help you. Embrace them.

To a certain degree, you need to think about time management. If you find a blog gushing over your music, do a little research on them first by checking their site ranking on Alexa.com, their number of Twitter followers and/or Facebook friends, and also the number of general commenters on their site. If you have endless energy (and some people working for you), maybe you can reach out to everyone. In the early stages, every mention is gold. As you gain stature, blogs that reach only a couple dozen people are probably not going to grow your audience quickly, and you may choose to be more judicious with your time.

I like to concentrate on people who appear to have 500 to 5,000 followers. Generally, this indicates that they are a "tastemaker" and exert a certain level of influence. However, they are small enough that they don't get 1,000 emails a day from artists pitching themselves. This increases the likelihood that they will respond to you, especially since they've already written favorably about you.

For sites that have much larger fanbases (such as the big music blogs), you certainly want to reach out to them, while also being realistic. These sites, which are getting pitches from thousands of bands, may not be as responsive. Therefore, focus on the individual writer of that blog entry and not the blog itself. There may be a dozen or more people writing for the site, but you don't have to be friends with all of them. You just need to reach the ones who like you the most and, therefore, will likely be your biggest champions.

Make sure that you regularly (at least once a week) update your site to include all these mentions. No matter how big or small they are, keep a list of everyone who's ever written anything about you. From an archiving perspective, you'll be glad you kept a running tally of all the nice things said about you. From a growth perspective, you want to establish reciprocity, promoting those that promote you. Each time you link back to that person's website, their site becomes slightly more likely to show up in a Google search result, just as their writing does for you. If a site turned someone on to your band, then you should at least attempt to turn your fans on to that site. Support the writers and fans that support you.

The same goes for your social networks. Facebook and Twitter updates also are drivers that can increase results in search rankings. They are almost certainly going to get more eyeballs than your website's press section.

As obvious as all of this is, it's less commonly deployed than you'd think. Many artists and bands just collect the alerts and archive them. They fail to build a relationship with those who talked fondly of them. Here's a secret of every artist who became an enduring star: They all remember the people who wrote positively about them in the early days. Start now, and not only will you cement a long-term bond, but you'll also put yourself ahead of at least half of the other artists written about on those sites. In other words, you'll gain a true fan that also happens to wield a megaphone.

But why stop there? As an artist, you want to go the extra mile, traveled by probably fewer than 2% of all musicians. I know this because, when I speak at conferences, I first ask who in the audience uses alerts. Most of the room raises a hand. Then I ask who uses this next hack, and usually only one person raises a hand. If you want to enter territory where very few people go and get important people to pay attention to you, set up Google Alerts for the three artists you most sound like.

What's the payoff for doing that? You immediately gain an ongoing active list of writers who have a high likelihood of liking your music, especially if they write about those artists regularly. These people, with audiences big and small, are all waxing poetic about an artist you feel you are similar to. At your stage of development, where every fan counts, targeting someone reasonably likely to enjoy your music that writes to an audience is the simplest action you can take.

You know who is usually appreciative of this? The writer you are communicating with. Google Alerts are not discriminatory, though they will likely rank results based on reach. Many of the people you are contacting are just getting into blogging or haven't reached a mass scale yet. Many of them will fall into that 500-to-5,000-person audience – a strong tastemaker zone for you. These people also cruise under the radar of most publicists, who generally only have time for more established bloggers. So while the major bands get worked to "theaters and arenas," you can do the hard work of visiting the "clubs" frequented by people truly in the know.

These writers appreciate that you're paying attention to them. You'd be thrilled to get a comment from a fan talking about how he listened to your music and loved it, right? Writers are the same. When you write them and say that you liked their piece on Bruno Mars, and because your music appeals to Bruno Mars's fans, you thought they'd like to hear it, they are more likely to give you a listen. That personal appeal stands out nearly every time.

When I get music from artists or bands, at least 90% of the requests are generic. It may be a press release, a standard servicing to various targets. It may even be a personal request to check out music, but it offers no personal details to indicate an effort to seek me out over anyone else. A very small fraction will specifically talk to *me*. I can tell they sent me music because they knew enough about me to believe I might like it and therefore could be helpful to their career. I listen to these submissions every time.

The hack here is the pitch. That is, the artist (or publicist) focused on giving me something that I'd like. Most artists focus on what *they* need. What they often fail to realize is that I don't need to promote any artist. Their request for a blog entry, record review or interview fails to move me. I need to know that someone cared to send me something that might improve my life or my product in some way, something that may get my audience excited. If they do, they are likely to be rewarded.

Writing personally to the writer appeals to their ego (in a good way) and gets them to pay attention faster. It doesn't mean that they are automatically going to like it. However, it does mean that they are more likely to give your music a try, and that's all you can really ask for. This hack also increases your chances for success with more prominent writers. When a writer gets hit up by a hundred bands a week, but only three or four people care enough to personally target them, whom do you think they'll check out first?

When you're determining those artists that you sound like, are you choosing big, mass-appeal artists or smaller artists who are still bigger than you? You should do both. It's easy for someone to say they like Sara Bareilles. A bit more interesting is to find someone who likes Brandi Carlile. A really interesting discovery is finding someone who likes Katie Herzig. A female indie-folk-pop artist is likely to appeal to fans of all three of those artists. Of the three, Katie Herzig might have the fewest things written about her, but the writer who gets an email about what they wrote about her will be impressed the most.

If you are serious about making it, responding to these alerts isn't something to do once in awhile; it should be a daily activity. Even the smallest opportunity can have a significant impact. Timeliness matters, and every step is a helpful one. No, not every request based on this method will be successful, but this hack offers a solid success rate and costs you only your time.

DON'T SEND ATTACHMENTS

After careful investigation, you've finally targeted the person who shows potential for liking or even buying your music. Maybe you've already had some contact with this individual, and she is receptive to hearing it. So you write an email with a couple of great lines about you, attach a few MP3s, and hit send.

You attached an MP3? Oh no!

OK, attaching a file is not *that* disastrous. Doing it won't suddenly destroy your career. I can tell you, though, that music professionals generally hate it. But because more musicians attach MP3s than provide an alternate listening method, you gain another opportunity to step ahead of many artists by appearing more professional than most to the person you are looking to impress. Not attaching an MP3 may not seem like a big thing, but it's a significant little hack that has a cumulative effect. For one can only get a hit if that hit is actually heard by enough people, especially by those who are influential.

It wouldn't seem this way. After all, a majority of people have high-speed Internet connections. Hard drives on computers have an insane amount of storage space. So what's the big deal about downloading a 5MB MP3? It's a 20 second download that takes up barely any space.

Well, the truth is that it's a pain in the ass. First, most artists don't know anything about metadata. More about metadata in a chapter solely on that subject, but one point is important to mention now: If you don't properly label your artist name, song title and all pertinent info into the metadata, the file gets lost in the hard drive. This is a perennial mistake of musicians, dating back to when demo tapes and CDs were lovingly put together, only to fail to include a contact name and number. I used to have a hard drive with about 100 songs that I have no idea who performed them. They came just as described. Note how I said *used to*!

The downloaded file inevitably becomes clutter on my hard drive that I just want to get rid of. I also don't want to have to perform two extra actions just to hear a song I didn't ask for in the first place. The first action is the download itself; the second is deleting said download. Together, they reliably trigger a negative reaction.

However, my clutter is nothing compared to that which burdens professional club DJs. They scream the most about attached downloads. They bring their laptops to the club, and the last thing they want is their professional equipment gummed up with unfamiliar, unsolicited songs they won't play. You might think that the DJ having the download on their hard drive improves your chances of being played, but the reality is that it just increases the chances he will get pissed off at you.

Now envision that you are an active music professional who uses Gmail to get all of your material. Many people are sending you music every week. You keep some backups of music you've sent out, and there's a lot of hi-res files of website mockups, flyers, etc. trading back and forth. All of a sudden, that 10GB hard drive doesn't seem so roomy. Guess which emails will be deleted first? I regularly sort by size and delete any unsolicited emails of 1MB or more.

So you get the deal that attaching downloads is counterproductive. So what's the hack? This is where the vast array of streaming options comes into play.

The service you use to stream matters far less than simply making sure that you do stream. If the file is small enough, an embedded streaming player within the email is a decent idea. That way, the listener doesn't have to jump to a website. The waiting time before the song plays is brief, because another page doesn't need to load. There's also something inherently pleasing about hitting a play button to get right to the music.

For many reasons, Soundcloud is a popular option. The player's flexibility allows you to do whatever is most comfortable. You can embed the player in the email. You can also just link out to the website and a page containing only the song or songs you want to present. Most important, you can also enable the player to allow for a download of the song right from the player.

Yes, I just got finished ranting about writers, DJs and other decision makers not wanting a download. That's true. The difference here is that the person on the other end controls the option to download or not. The music professional hates it when the only way to hear the suggested music is via download. However, if they like it, they will very likely *want* a download. It's better to give them the choice to do it at that moment. If they have to send you an email to request it, they usually won't bother.

The download option allows you to keep track of statistics, which can be valuable for you in determining whether people actually like your song. If you see a download number that's close to the stream count, it's a good bet that your song is being well received. However, if you find your song has been streamed several hundred times, but has only one download (hi, mom!), then maybe you need to push another song.

When you send download files, you have no way of tracking that song's success rate. You could send it out to 100 people and have no idea whether all or none of them heard it. On the other hand, I can gauge the success of a pitch anytime by monitoring the stream counts after sending it out. If the stream count exceeds the number of emails sent, this is an encouraging sign. It almost certainly means there's some degree of viral action. With a site like Yousendit, I can see if the person I specifically sent it to downloaded it. They can't hide from those stats.

Your song may be great, but your pitch could be bad. To check for this possibility, put together several streaming links. There's nothing preventing you from putting the same song up several times, even on the same service. This technique directs people to different streams according to the particular pitch. You can see if one email performs better than another. The more successful pitch can be the one you distribute across the board, accompanied, of course, by the personal touch.

All of these techniques carry over to social networking, as well. Tweeting and posting about free downloads in this environment is all well and good. For people who are already fans of yours, they are going to respond favorably to your offer. However, for the people you are attempting to reach, a YouTube streaming link is much more effective. It's the same logic. They don't want unfamiliar content cluttering their music folder. And don't forget to track the different pitches here, too, either by unique short links or separate streaming links.

A bonus hack, which may not dramatically help but also won't hurt, is to include a separate streaming link containing only the hook of your song. I've heard of a few publishers who are doing this to allow the listener either to listen to the hook right away, without plodding through an entire song, or to have the hook at the ready for easy reference if they like the song. This may be an odd choice for your pitch to actual fans, but when approaching the industry, it can only help. At worst, it will be ignored, and if so, at least your email will carry a message that you understand the mechanics of the industry. Those subtleties go a long way toward separating you from the amateurs.

I will look forward to receiving emails from people who have read this book and were inspired enough to ask me to check out their music. If you send me a link to a stream or embedded player, you're in. But if you attach an MP3, don't be offended when I automatically delete that file. At least you were warned.

ALWAYS PROMOTE THOSE THAT PROMOTE YOU

The Golden Rule. I actually heard that a social networking musician originally wrote this rule. I believe the rule at that time read, "Promote unto others as they promote unto you." Or maybe I'm just delusional.

Either way, this is a great hack to hold onto and live by as long as you can. The world of social networking is really all about reciprocity. If all you do is receive adoration, eventually you will get a negative reputation. Remember, everyone is now a broadcaster. If you do something that inadvertently upsets people, they could respond either by saying negative things about you, or worse, choose to ignore you from that point forward.

If you genuinely like what someone does, don't just link to it. Talk glowingly about that person and what they did. Chances are the person will remember you for a long time. In this high-tech world, "high touches" like that can go a long way when you're hopeful that someone will write about your song.

If you don't like what someone does, don't lie and pretend you love them. Just acknowledge them with a simple thank you. The act of just recognizing what they wrote for you tends to be enough. In the Twitter world, this can easily be done by taking the person's tweet about you and retweeting it with a "Thank you!" right in front of it. Takes two seconds.

An easy way to lump together many acknowledgements is through the "Follow Friday" Internet meme. You may have seen this online when someone lists a bunch of screen names with a "#FF" at the beginning or end. This is an easy, efficient way to acknowledge those that acknowledged you. And there's no rule that says you can only do one tweet's worth of promoting. Make the effort to recognize more people and post several times on Friday. Just don't do it every hour, as there is a risk of overkill.

For those who adopted social networking early, reciprocal kudos and links are almost second nature. However, you have an opportunity to expand this to everything you do.

Live gigs are often forgotten as a place to thank people. Again, always good to be mindful of overkill, but shout-outs from the stage go a long way toward cementing a bond with fans or music business professionals. You might be thanking them for the blog entry they wrote to bring people to the show. Maybe they made a shirt by hand proclaiming their love for you. Perhaps they are the only one in the bar. Don't look at yourself as too cool for the room. Nothing is cooler to a fan than a shout-out.

A fundamental reason for doing this is literally right in front of everyone's faces: Everyone wants to be loved and noticed. Saying "thank you" in private is certainly appreciated. However, if someone did something very publicly for you, then a reciprocal public acknowledgement is a powerful statement by you to that person.

Especially in the early stages of a career, the one thing every artist needs is a fan who will talk about him or her to anyone and everyone. Give those fans a story, and they will tell even more people. The person I've seen do this better than anyone is Taylor Swift. She's gone out of her way in multiple settings to thank those who have helped her. She has done this several times with me personally over the years, making me a fan for life. One time, though, stands out. Backstage at the Academy of Country Music Awards in Las Vegas in 2011, Taylor had just won Entertainer of the Year. While navigating the press gauntlet, she saw me and came over to say a quick hello. Not only did she thank me for my support, she also congratulated *me* for an award I had won a *month* earlier, something extremely minor compared to the huge honor just bestowed upon her. That she actually remembered she wanted to recognize me at that moment was stunning. Needless to say, I've recounted that story dozens of times, not to stroke myself but because I want people to know how great a person I think Taylor is. This book gives me another opportunity to do that.

Don't just limit your prop-swapping to fans. Do it with artists, too. Each artist, no matter the size of his or her Facebook and Twitter lists, is a broadcaster. If you say something nice about another artist, your fans will respect the recommendation. Naturally, you would get the same in return if another artist mentioned you. Artists who do interact with each other and reciprocate mentions of each other form bigger audiences faster and forge stronger bonds with like-minded artists.

One example I remember is when a group of singer/songwriters took this to an extreme that only grew everyone's fanbase. These artists decided to band together for a tour, but they didn't stop there. To promote the tour, they each decided to each record a cover version of a song by another artist on the tour. This gave fans of Artist A an even more meaningful reason to check out Artist B, because Artist B was playing Artist A's song. Brilliant!

For years, many artists have understood the power of recording with other artists to trade off fanbases. They don't even need to be in the same state. These artists write together online; then one artist records some tracks and sends them to the other to overlay their part. Many of these artists also record separate videos of themselves performing the song, and then one of them edits the videos together. They may never be physically together during the entire process. Yet their fans can feel the connection, and each artist will watch their own audience grow as a result.

There are countless examples of artists helping one another. This may even seem less of a hack and more of an obvious 'good person" thing. That may be, but because there are so many acts that don't do this, there's no question its inclusion in this book is warranted. Is it amazing that just by being nice, you could rise to a level above most artists? I think so, but that's the way it is. So just do as an artist what your mama (I hope) told you to do as a person. Slowly but surely, the goodwill will pay off throughout your career.

GO MOBILE

Back in 1999, I saw many a musician resist putting their music online. After all, CDs were selling through the roof. So why would you put something online? For free, no less! A bit more than a decade later, I think you know why.

Now we're in an age where many teenagers are already increasingly forgoing the Web. An email address used to be a major communication device. Now it's something that exists just to enable registrations. Everyone can see how intelligent and fast smart phones have become; yet artists fail to recognize its impact on the music they create.

By taking a few simple steps, you can make sure your music is accessible through this important new means of distribution. The difficulty is that the cellular world is a somewhat more controlled environment than the Web-connected PC or laptop. This is by the phone manufacturers' own design. That's OK, because what you do will be more prominent. Don't be daunted by the task of putting things up on the Web for the mobile market.

Let's start with apps, which seem insurmountable to many. Yet if you have a website and paid someone to put that together, why wouldn't you do the same thing for an app? Remember, the last thing you want to be is invisible. So do you want someone to search in an app store for your band name and find…nothing? Of course not.

So you can certainly pay someone to design something for you much like a website. However, maybe you designed your website from a free template, and didn't worry about paying for anything other than the hosting costs. But did you know you could do the same thing for an app? Although several companies offer this service, I'm partial to Mobile Roadie. There is a cost, but it's based on how much people use the app. If that's just 10 people, we're talking pocket change.

My advice would be to not charge for the app. Because you're reading this book, chances are your brand name is still, shall we say, "accruing value." Even if you make it big, consider that nearly all major music stars who have platinum albums do not charge for their apps. So it'd be hard for you to justify asking a consumer to spend more on your app than for a superstar's. Even Angry Birds, the insanely addictive popular game, only costs 99 cents. When you are more popular and entertaining than that, go ahead and charge something.

Don't worry that people won't use your app much. Most apps are something people use for a day or two, and then delete or forget about. This is true even for the most engaging band apps. That's OK. Your goal here is to help a potential fan get to know you a bit better, even for a brief moment. However disposable your app may be, it improves your visibility and helps ensure that that fans can connect with you when they want to. If your music is as good as you feel it is, you will retain those fans through other means.

Having said that, remember to keep your app updated. I realize it's a huge pain in the ass. You've already got to update a website, a Twitter feed, a Facebook feed, a Reverbnation page, etc. It's not easy to keep your music active at all levels of the game, but you must provide momentum and sustain it. That gives you a competitive advantage over the slackers.

Remember that the $10 a month on Web hosting and $10 for mobile are an inevitable part of the price you pay to do business in the music world. In the grand scheme of things, spending these sums to make sure someone can find you isn't incredibly expensive.

Of course, mobile is not just about the apps world. Millions of people access traditional websites on their smartphones. Unfortunately, something that looks and works fine on a PC monitor or laptop is another story on a 2" mobile screen. Yes, you can pinch and zoom, but most people won't do that unless they *really* want the content they're getting. So you have to make sure that your website looks good on a mobile device. When you're talking to your Web designer, this should be a primary objective.

For starters, make sure that your home page is not overloaded with crap. Dump that dumb Flash movie. iPhones don't run Flash technology. So if someone types in www.yourbandhere.com on their iPhone and gets your Flash movie, he sees a black screen. He's not likely to say, "Hey, I better get myself to a computer to see the awesome Flash movie this band created." No, he moves to the next thing and forgets about your band. For that matter, this applies to anything Flash on your page. When something doesn't work on a Website, it's a reflection on you, not the Web designer or the person on the other end who doesn't realize it's a technology issue.

For the same basic reason, don't put in every bit of information about your band on your home page. On a tiny screen, it's all going to look like mush. Pick the few important things and leave it at that: A pertinent piece of news, a tour date or two, the nicest photo (but not 10 of them!). As they say, keep it simple, stupid.

If you're in the mood to spend money on Facebook ads, why not spend a little on mobile ads? At some point in a few years, this market will be very cluttered. But at the moment, there's not nearly as many people spending. Even with usage as big as it is, there is a huge inventory available, which makes mobile advertising cheap! We like cheap to hack hits!

Apps, web pages and mobile ads are great, but they pale in comparison to the simplicity of text messages. Texting by adults is skyrocketing, while teens send and receive 100 texts a day.

How often are you texting your fans? I hope not that often, because the last thing you want is for them to think of you as a spammer. However, you should figure out once a week the most important thing you need to communicate to your fans and then text it out there. It's safe to text out shortlinks to your new videos, free downloads, or other sites for which you need to boost traffic. Now that so many people have smartphones, clicking on the links from a text message makes it easy to get to the content.

Put together a list of your most important followers and keep it handy. When that important message is ready to text out, you've already got the mailing list ready to go. If you haven't compiled your fans' mobile numbers, just ask them. If some don't give it to you, that's OK. Be happy with whatever you do get. The bottom line is that if you have an email list to send to, a Facebook "like" list to message and a Twitter list to tweet to, you should also have a text list. You'd be amazed how many artists don't.

By the way, you may want to add an extra phone number to your current cell plan just to exchange text messages with fans. You obviously don't want fans to have your "real" cell phone number. So spend an extra $20 a month to have a separate number for them. Have it automatically go to voicemail, and check the messages every couple of days. Then, when you're out at dinner, you can have that phone safely stored in a gear case and your real phone won't interrupt your dinner with callers telling you how your music is helping them get over a significant other who just dumped them.

One last thing: How many times do you see phones raised in the air at your show? All the time? If there's one thing you can guarantee, it's that nearly everyone in your concert crowd now has a cell phone. It is an instant connection to your fan you should use. Don't waste time having the friend roaming the floor with a clipboard asking people to sign up to a mailing list. You can do it quickly and easily from the stage with the use of their phones.

Have them text your fan phone number so you can collect their numbers to text back to them. Make sure you tell the audience that you'll text them back from time to time. Offer free download cards or t-shirts as incentives by selecting numbers at random. When they text, ask them to text their email addresses so you can aggregate to those, too.

The smartphone is, of course, much more than a database collection tool. Encourage fans to take pictures during a particular song and to post them to their Facebook wall or Twitter accounts, and you'll repost your favorites.

Think of it this way: Tell them to sing, and they sing along. Tell them to dance, and they get up and start dancing. Wave your hands in the air, and they do that, too. So why not give them an action that spreads the word about you? If you tell them, for example, to tell their friends where they are, they probably will. You could go from two Facebook posts from people about being at your show to 20. With pictures showing how cool you are.

That smartphone is way more powerful than most people think. Every time you see it at a show in a fan's hand, it's an opportunity. This is both the most ubiquitous device in use right now, and the most under-utilized when it comes to fan interaction. Don't take it for granted. Use it to your advantage to spread the word.

BOY, THIS IS A LOT TO MANAGE

I'm not gonna lie to you. This book presents a lot of ideas and techniques to implement. You may already be feeling overwhelmed. There's so much for you to do that doesn't even involve creating the music itself. Let's pause for two important points:

First, don't feel overwhelmed. You really don't have to do everything, and even if you want to, you don't have to do it all at once. Just as you would schedule a day in the studio, schedule a day for yourself to market your music. Block out everything else and hit each idea one by one. Work your way through your individual tasks, and you will achieve a lot.

Second, you need to commit to this level of dedication and time to put into your work if you want to have a hit. I know very few successful artists who aren't working 24/7 at their career. If you can't put in the time to market, as well as to create, it's unlikely a hit will be coming your way. That's just reality.

Having said that, a hack is, to some degree, supposed to cut out a lot of hard work. If you really get into what each of these tips is about, these hacks will save you an immense amount of time. But there's still a lot of tough efforts ahead.

So, don't get discouraged. Take it step by step. Work the ideas methodically. Recognize that even one of these tips, applied properly and fully, will give you a significant step up from the hundreds of thousands of new artists each year trying to catch a break.

You can do it. You can hack.

COMMENTS

Commenting is everywhere. It's on message boards, iTunes and social networks. It's on news articles, and even on your mom's refrigerator. (Because you forgot to take out the trash, didn't you?) And wherever they appear, comments have impact. An effective comment on a message board can yield a days-long discussion. A positive comment on iTunes might result in a download. A comment on a social network post might lead to a stronger bond between the poster and the commenter. The news article gains more definition as part of a discussion.

Let's be honest. You may not always comment, but you generally read them. Perhaps not in depth, because you've got a million things going on. But more often than not, you'll take a five-second glance. If for nothing else, you're subconsciously gauging what the world thinks of something. No longer can you have someone ask, "Did you hear about Band X?" and reply, "Yes, but I don't know much, so please tell me more." Now when someone says, "Did you hear about Band X?" you have to say, "Yes, and I heard that the new record isn't that great." To say otherwise means you're out of the social conversation. Never mind the fact that you gleaned this opinion from glancing at the comments after you read something while surfing around. You didn't listen to the music, but still formed an opinion. If you can't admit you do it around music (and I know you do, but I'll forgive you), then think about it for the latest film coming out or a TV show. See? I knew you did it. We all do.

But here's the interesting part about that. Most people don't comment. And I don't mean seven out of 10 people. It's more like 99 out of 100. As a test, I selected at random 25 YouTube videos that had been promoted to me. These videos covered a broad range of exposure – from as low as 500 views to more than 4 million. The average percentage of commenters to total views was 0.38%, or about four per thousand.

Of course, my sample was unscientific. That said, the highest comment rate any one video received was only 1.45%. You get the point. People are passive, but they do eavesdrop. While they don't comment, they at least glance at the comments, because they want to know the conversation.

This means your video with low views is actually in danger of having no comments. While my sample didn't come across any in that situation, there were some with a rate that rounded out to 0.00%. That essentially means ... (insert sound of crickets here). We've all seen pieces of content with no comments. When we do, we think nobody cares about it. It's the equivalent of eating in a restaurant and being the only diner. It doesn't matter if a lot of people are there on another night. You feel like a loser, being where other people aren't.

The obvious solution is to make sure that all of your content – music, blogs, all of it – has comments associated with it. But how do you get those comments? What's the hack? Simple – you leave a comment. I hope you're prepared to say something nice about yourself! And get over any feelings of embarrassment about this. This is the music business, and something like this will likely be the least shameful thing you do. After all, if you don't talk positively about your music, who will?

Now, some evident rules on your own commenting: Don't use your own name; you never want to look too obvious. Don't talk about your album in a way that's too gushing or over the top. No one is likely to believe you are as good as Nirvana's *Nevermind*, so avoid comparing yourself with icons. Just keep it simple, short and to the point about how good the music is.

Comment everywhere you can. Many people won't comment because they don't want to be the only one at the party. Other people long to comment first, but they are a smaller subset of an already-small subset. So anywhere you see something about you, make sure to leave a comment. When it's a site that offers a wide range of content, such as iTunes, make it generic, such as, "Amazing live show. Song X is a killer." If it's a more specific site – for example, a blog post about your record – feel free to comment as yourself and thank the writer. I know, the writing really wasn't that good, and he misinterpreted your song, but man, wasn't it a great article?

So now you've commented. What else do you do? If you're in a band, make sure your other band members comment, too. Everyone's gotta pull their fair share of the weight. If the drummer wants equal songwriting credit because he was in the room at the time the song was written, he must be willing to leave as many comments as you do. If your band absolutely had to have that second guitarist, then he can sure leave a second comment.

Next, move on to those who love you best – your friends and family. Be forewarned that they may gush just a wee bit too much. That's OK in the scheme of things, but you should advise them to stay within reasonable bounds. No need for Uncle Roger to talk about bouncing you on his knee when you were three years old. That's not good for the hack. Just have him say, "Love their music. Can't wait to hear more," and leave it at that. If you're really ambitious and want to control the message, write individual things for your family to post, so all they have to do is copy and paste.

After that, ask your fans. The size of your mailing list is irrelevant. This is just like asking people to dance at your show or text you their info. Remember, many of your fans are waiting for you to ask them to do something, so oblige them. Will all of them take you up on it? No, but some will, and that's all you need.

At some point, you'll have enough fans that you won't have to do this all the time. By then, they will be active all on their own and will take care of this for you. Until then, it's incumbent on you to make sites look as if you have a very active fan base. Ask everyone you can think of to comment. It will only be a short while before many more will want to join the party.

READ DEREK SIVERS' BOOK

On his website, Derek Sivers offers the following:

A free e-book with my best advice for my fellow musicians, about how to be more successful promoting your music.
It's a combination of my advice from my own experience, and my advice from watching the experiences of other successful musicians.
I don't want to sell my advice. I just want musicians to succeed. So - feel free to pass this around to anyone. Email it to your friends. Paste it into your blog or bulletin board.
Enter your info, and the PDF e-book will be emailed to you immediately.

In case you don't know Derek, he started CD Baby, the first company to allow any musician to sell their music online. In 1997, well before iTunes, his site operated with the rather simple philosophy that anyone could enroll and start retailing their music. His role was, in fact, a necessary step that led to aggregators such as Tunecore and The Orchard, which help independent artists distribute their music across the Web.

Derek sold CD Baby in 2008 for millions, which afforded him a lifestyle that allows him to speak his mind. He doesn't rabble-rouse so much as inspire. If he's giving you time, he's probably giving you advice. His advice should be obvious, yet it's not.

His book takes maybe 45 minutes to read, is easy to digest and is engrossing. His pointers are as much about simple life lessons as they are about hacks to grow your music career. I'm sure I absorbed some of his ideas into other chapters of this book and reconstituted them into new angles. Others are so simple that it's hard to say whether I absorbed them from Derek or just always knew them.

Derek has also written a very good book for sale called *Anything You Want*. It includes 200 song downloads as a bonus. To get started, though, read his free book. If you don't follow those credos, no hack in this book will be enough. Since his book is so minimalist, I will keep his chapter brief in its honor, and just recommend that you go get it. Now.

http://sivers.org/pdf

TARGET FANS WITH KLOUT

http://klout.com/

What is Klout? Klout measures your overall online impact on a scale of 1 to 100. It looks at Twitter, Facebook, etc. and examines several factors. It looks at your True Reach, or how big your engaged audience is. Another is Amplification Probability, or how likely it is that a person in your audience will click your link. Then there's your Network Influence, such as how often you get retweeted. All told, these metrics can measure exactly how influential you are.

Why do you need to know this? Because having a hit is not just how you write and record a song. It's also *how well* you get that hit out there. You probably understand the power of Twitter and Facebook in spreading the word about your music, but what are you *really* doing about it?

Klout's not the only one offering this measurement service. A new site called PeerIndex also registers influence, using a variety of additional factors singling out your industry. Several of my colleagues now are tracking their PeerIndex ranking, which suggests it's gaining traction.

I've thought a lot about Klout because how much you have of it is crucial to how successful you may be. I created posts on Rebecca Black that were intended to illustrate why it became a hit. But I also knew that her trending, combined with my analysis, would likely reach a broader audience. This, in turn, raises my Klout and expands my influence. I try to be judicious about the number of people I follow in ratio to the people who follow me. A ratio that's too high will lower my Klout, and thus diminish my influence.

As an artist, how do you use your Klout? Do you "manage yourself" to maintain great influence, or are you spreading yourself wide but thin? Consider the Klout of those who follow you. A September 2010 article in *AdAge* reported on how several companies find fans with Klout and target them with perks. This is some of the smartest targeted marketing you can do. It's the kind of thing musicians used to do well, but have since let slide.

Indeed, the underpinning of technologies such as Klout and PeerIndex is a philosophy: Treat the *most influential* fans well, and watch your fanbase grow. Not hard to understand.

In an ideal world, you would want to treat your fans equally. But if you want to be successful, you just can't do that right now, except perhaps before or after a show. That's the time to be gracious and polite to everyone who approaches you. (It's not bad, though, to have a person nearby who can remind you that "you have somewhere to be" when someone just won't stop talking to you. Remember, you can never be perceived as the bad guy. Let a manager or publicist do it. That's part of the reason you pay them.)

But for controlling the everyday interaction with fans, which covers most of your week, you need to prioritize your time. To hack your hit, spend your time with the people who have the highest likelihood of spreading a positive word about your music. When you're going about your daily business of making music, it's often difficult to ascertain whom those people are. That's why it's important to learn how to recognize this with as little effort as possible.

Your daily routine should include spending time with those who reach out to you with the greatest frequency. Some of these key people are obsessive fans who can't stop talking about you. Rethink any aversion you may have to them, because they'll only become more plentiful as you get hits. However, you do need to be strategic as you deal with these people. On a scale of 1 to 100, their devotion might be pinging the meter at 100, but their influence might be a 1 if they're an obsessive loner.

When fans you don't know come up to you in a concert, the only gauge you have to their influence is the number of people they are with. If they've brought 10 of their friends, they are probably what you'd call a social connector. If they appear to be shy and on their own, then you can make a good, if imperfect, guess on where they stand. Online, however, we have plenty of metrics to gauge their real influence.

A simple way to do this is to see how many friends each individual has. The more friends they have, the more you are likely to want to interact with them. However, if they have 2,000 friends, but rarely update them with their activity, then they're not really that valuable for your purposes, at least online. Meanwhile, a person who has 500 friends and communicates with them several times a day or week likely has more influence. Klout scores parse this information for you quickly and efficiently.

Once you harvest information on the most influential fans, make sure you separate them from your other mailing lists. Treat them like the A-list people they deserve to be. Give them extra offerings you might not extend to other fans. Since they're more social, offer them 2-for-1 passes to your show, to encourage them to bring people to the show with them and, in turn, strengthen their influence further. Have a deal where, if they bring three friends to the show, they get a t-shirt. Run a contest with this A-list group offering the person who tweets your message the most a free house concert. Don't be shy with this group. They can do big things for you.

This is also the group you should proactively reach out to from time to time. Don't just treat them like a specialized mailing list that gets more offers. Make time at least once a month to send each of them a personalized message. Don't look at this as a burden. These people *should* be your best friends. At the early stage of your career, the momentum provided by as little as a few dozen people could establish the difference between having major hits and no hits.

Try to identify two to three key people in each city where you are gaining fans and plan to perform. But don't just reach out to them twice a year when you're playing in that town. People can see right through that. Instead, keep up the personal communication with them every month. It's important that you reach out to them at times when you have nothing much going on. In fact, make it a point to ask about *their* lives. That's what friends do, and that's what you need to be doing.

Having trouble remembering personal information? Keep a contacts list or mailing list, and take notes. Write down the names of their boyfriends and girlfriends. Their pets. If they're a vegetarian or a gun nut. Any bit of information that could be important. You'd be amazed how much further fan devotion will go if you can recall (even by email) a tiny piece of inconsequential information much later. They'll know you were listening.

I know one artist who, at an early stage in his career, offered his top 100 fans a lifetime backstage pass. Sure, this artist was only playing clubs where there was no security to the backstage, but the point was that he identified his hardcore early fans and gave them a badge of honor that had real meaning. It was only 100 people (and they were numbered) so even if he became an arena star years later, the total would still be manageable. Think about how excited people become when they get a virtual badge from a random site. Now exponentially increase that when it's a physical item with real value.

The key hack here is to identify people not just by their devotion, but also by their influence. If you have a fanbase of 200 loners, your audience will grow by 0. If you have an audience of 200 social butterflies, your audience starts growing by multiples. It's up to you to sort these fans out and focus on the ones who will grow that base the fastest. These extra few minutes will shave off years on the time it takes you to become a hit artist.

PROMOTE TO NICHE SITES

Do you know how many artists are promoting to pure music sites like Pitchfork? Nearly all of them. Certainly way more than they have room to promote. Do you know how many artists are promoting to non-music sites that appeal to a specific lifestyle? Very few.

I like to spend my time in areas where the odds are stacked as much in my favor as possible. At some point, the odds will improve with a site like Pitchfork. That will happen after I've been able to assemble a decent portion of the conversation and amass a solid following. Until then, there's actually a better chance of getting picked up by a niche site than a music site.

When you're building your story of a hit record, it's important to recognize that stats like download sales and YouTube views don't discriminate based on where they come from. If your mom's site can motive 10,000 people from her group of macramé followers to watch your video, why wouldn't you take those views? A fan sees only the total number, not how the number was assembled. When you create a hit, you're creating an image. Record companies will do anything possible to create the perception of a hit, so why wouldn't you?

Your mom's macramé site would likely be a lucky accident. First, I didn't realize that your mom was that digitally savvy! Second, it'd be difficult for you to present your music to a macramé site where you don't know anyone, presuming that your band is not into macramé, your song is not about macramé or your video does not show off your mad macramé skillz. On the other hand, if you fulfill any of those three qualifications, then you should absolutely pitch the macramé site.

The key to getting these placements is the obvious context. If you can find a nice hook on how your song or band can connect with the site, then you've got your opening. If you have a cult following of horror film buffs, then it only makes sense to track down a site that specializes in that audience. If your song uses Druid stone circles as a metaphor for your relationship, why not find the sites that specialize in this subject matter?

These sites are not usually getting hit up much by outsiders. Most of the time they communicate internally about all things related to their subject matter. Occasionally, some external company will pitch them on a promotion. For the most part, though, they are not targeted often and certainly are not pitched often by ambitious musicians (mostly because most musicians are not ambitious!). So, when put in that perspective, would you rather be one of 100 submissions that day, or the only submission that month? These niche sites give you much better odds.

Are all these sites going to respond positively by posting something on the site? Nope. But these sites have a much higher likelihood of actually listening to your music and paying attention. The music site is going to glance at your well-thought-out pitch letter and give your song 15 seconds to impress them. The niche site is going to be so intrigued as to why a musician thought a macramé site was a good target that there is a higher likelihood of their listening to the music.

Don't look for anything specific in return from these sites. Keep in mind that they probably don't have a music or general entertainment section. They are busy publishing only information that's relevant to their community, and music may not be a part of it. However, if the people you reach do like it, they have several ways of spreading the word. For one, it may not make it onto a blog, but it may make it as a post on their Facebook page. Perhaps they'll put out a tweet. Maybe they'll include your music as the cute little "and also in our world" section at the bottom of their emailed newsletter. Doesn't really matter. Any one of the above is more than you had prior to that moment.

Don't expect any earth-shattering traffic from these sites, either. Most niche sites really don't reach a big audience; that's why they're called niche sites. Just remember that it's a step forward in exposure. Every factor that contributes to your overall story is valuable. Those 50 views are not likely to generate more than any individual would produce via Twitter or a smaller music blog. So take it and smile. Who knows? Maybe one of those sites has bigger traffic than you expect. Or maybe another macramé site picks up on the placement from the first one and it starts to go viral. Don't underestimate where it could go.

Also, don't stop with either one site or one niche. This is something that can become meaningful if you start dealing with volume. Find as many sites as you deem directly relevant to your song or artistry and go after all of them. Then think of a secondary subject that pertains to your music and go after those sites. The Internet is infinite, and this exercise also can be infinite. Yes, at some point you'll need to stop, so don't strain too much to think of every possible angle. Move on to the next song. The key to this hack is remembering that you are in the process of getting as much exposure as possible and boosting your raw numbers.

Think of it this way: Many musicians spend a lot of time pimping their music to every TV show, hoping one of them will pick it up to play in the background. The show itself is irrelevant, but exposure and dollars from performance royalties do matter. This isn't much different. Play in the area where your odds of moving up the exposure ladder are much better than those given by inundated music supervisors.

WATCH YOUR OWN DAMN VIDEO

This one seems self-explanatory, but it's not. The number of artists who don't watch their video, and watch it often, astounds me. After all, can you expect someone to do something that you wouldn't do yourself?

I realize that by the time you've completed the process of making a video, you're probably feeling a touch too close to it. That's OK. Watch it anyway. It's also a smart idea to watch it just to make sure everything uploaded properly. You'd be surprised how many times content that artists thought went up fine experienced difficulties.

You may also think that in a world of millions of video views, your one individual view doesn't really mean anything. After all, to get a million views, your one view amounts to only 0.0001%. On the other hand, many people think something is legitimately going on with your song once there are at least 1,000 views. Because most don't even reach 100, every view counts. So watch your video as often as possible.

There's only one reason for you to hold back on watching it nonstop. YouTube can track your user ID or IP address and notice when you've watched the video over and over from one location. They look down on such practice because they don't want hackers manipulating their metrics.

The proliferation of devices, however, almost makes this a moot point. You can easily rack up dozens of views before any automated system could ever catch on. If ever. It's all about how tactical you are as you do it.

Before I explain how to do this, keep one thing in mind: Make sure you are unregistered each time you do it. Log out of your YouTube account before you start racking up views. It's OK if a view or two happens within your account. They won't ever boot you off for attempting to watch your video over and over. They just will not count the numbers. In order for the views to accumulate for you, stay logged off. Make sure you also delete your cookies to minimize their tracking abilities.

Now, how do you rack up these views? The easy answer, of course, is to watch the video on as many devices in as many locations as you can. For example, I can watch on my home computer. My wife's computer. Her iPhone. My iPad. My office computer. Or on two Web-connected televisions. That's seven views, and I'm just getting started.

Every time you are in a new wi-fi hotspot, watch your video, because in each hotspot, you should get a new IP address. YouTube is more concerned about the bots that would jack up the view count by hundreds over a very short period. With this hack, we're talking about getting a relatively very low number of views over many days. No, doing this is not by itself going to get you a hit song. But in a world where every view counts, why wouldn't you do this?

Don't worry that the view count does not increase every time you watch a video. This is part of YouTube's efforts to keep the view counts legit. After your video has been watched 300 times, the system will only update it periodically so that YouTube can validate the numbers. The more devices you use, the more legit your views will be.

Which, by the way, is also a sneaky way to get your views up wherever you go. Why limit it to only the devices you own? With so many people owning portable devices, it's easier than ever to rack up a view *and* expose your music to your friend. Don't take no for an answer! Say, "Hey, have you seen my new video?" and then take their phone, load up YouTube and play it for them.

If you're really sophisticated, a super-legit tech hack involves switching your IP address to fool YouTube into thinking you're a different computer. I won't go into detail about how to do it, since it's very techie and time-consuming. However, if you're ambitious, go online and find out details about proxy switching. Yes, you'll find a lot of people who also supposedly do this to garner YouTube views. That doesn't mean you *have* to do it to achieve success.

What I will caution you to avoid are automatic programs that charge you to set up automated YouTube views. These have proven to be notoriously unreliable, are not inexpensive and are often caught by YouTube. A much better idea, if you're interested in going this route, is to learn about proxies and implement it yourself. It's cheaper and a bit more reliable.

I realize that these may be incremental to your video count, but you're at a point where they are important. While you shouldn't spend every hour of every day watching your own video, watch is as often as you can in as many places as possible. Of course, you don't have to actually be "watching" the video; let it run in the background. It's easy to add a dozen or so plays daily just by remembering to do it.

BUY YOUR OWN DAMN MUSIC

Buying your own downloads is much like watching your own video. If you're not going to do it, who else will? Granted, watching your own video is a little different, because doing that doesn't cost you anything. You log on, go to the website address and watch. Not a penny spent. Downloads are another matter. If you're going to buy your own music, it's going to cost you a dollar.

Or does it? You have to remember that this is *your* music. Let's assume that you're not signed to a big record company, and you placed the music up for sale yourself. This means, of course, that you get paid for each download. When you buy a 99-cent download, 70 cents comes back to you, so that download only costs you 29 cents. You'll spend 10 times that amount on a Starbucks coffee to wake yourself up before rehearsal.

But why should you buy your own music in the first place? One reason is logistical: it's quality control. You may have done everything you were supposed to with your digital distributor to get your music uploaded into their system. You tested and listened to the song, and it all sounded fine. However, in a world where the distributor is dealing with thousands of songs weekly and each service ingests tens of thousands of songs, errors can and do occur. One way to confirm that your music made it in there correctly and in one piece is by buying and listening to it yourself.

So, what difference does that one copy make? In the purest sense, not much. Just as with watching a video, buying a copy of your song takes you only 0.0001% of the way to becoming Platinum. But here's a startling fact: Now that most music is released independently, an overwhelming majority of titles fail to sell even 100 downloads. Looking at it another way, 100 copies will catapult you to the top percentile of independent musicians. So in a practical sense, one copy gets you 1% of your way there – a meaningful percentage.

Sounds great, except … people forget one thing. iTunes is, of course, not the only store that sells your music. In the US, you can also sell music on Amazon, Rhapsody, eMusic, Verizon, Nokia, Bandcamp, Music Unlimited and many more destinations. The Orchard aggregation service alone distributes music to 660 retail outlets in 75 countries!

Now, I wouldn't expect you to go around the world and buy from each outlet. That might be good and ambitious, but I'm not sure that will accomplish much. Also, for those of you reading outside of the US, I'm focused on the American market mostly because I know it best. I can't say for certain how much what I'm about to say applies to your market. For now, let's just assume that you are buying from US-based stores.

For most artists, despite demonstrating the ability to make something with online music, getting signed to a major record company is the ultimate goal. Labels study several metrics to ascertain whether or not an artist is having any significant impact. One of those is SoundScan, which combines all digital sales into one neat, easy-to-read format. If you want to impress record companies, your SoundScan tally needs to be of a decent size. Selling 100 copies on your own won't get you signed. However, since so few artists achieve this goal, 100 copies at least puts you on their radar if your music comes across their desk.

With that in mind, if you buy your music from 10 outlets in the US, you're now counted as 10 copies in SoundScan. That's 10% towards that first goal, and the net cost to you is only three dollars. Sacrifice one latte for one day. If you're in a band, get the other members to do it, too. Then, let's say everyone gets their boyfriend or girlfriend to do the same. In a four-piece band, you've now sold 80 copies. Suddenly, that first 100-copy hurdle doesn't seem so insurmountable. And this is before you start bugging your parents to do the same thing.

You can see how quickly this can add up. Spend 10 bucks now, get seven bucks back later, and improve the likelihood of showing up on record company radars. Even if you don't right away, you'll have a better story than most artists for a label to see once you do. Just give up the fancy coffee for a day.

Now, shall we go one level deeper? I think we shall! How about coordinating this effort so that everyone is buying your music on the same day? Perhaps the first day your music comes out. It's naturally a dream for everyone to get on those iTunes sales charts. However, iTunes comprises a huge majority of digital sales, so even one of its sub-charts is likely out of your grasp until you get some real momentum. On the other hand, the other sites don't get nearly as much traffic or sales. Most artists don't realize that people actually buy music on a subscription site like Rhapsody. Yet a sale on Rhapsody generates the same money as one on iTunes and looks exactly the same to a record company as an iTunes or SoundScan sale. And it could be a whole lot easier to appear on these charts, especially the sub-genre ones.

The beauty about claiming a chart position is that you only have to do it once. Many times you'll see an ad about the No. 1 movie in America. It may actually be No. 1 only for a week and then sink like a stone because the movie stinks. But they can never take away the fact that it was at one moment in time a No. 1 movie. Same thing with albums. I've seen many an album over the years debut at No. 1, only to plummet and be forgotten a month later. Those records may never sell much, but in a marketplace context, achieving that position is a key attribute that will attract attention.

My first book, *Futurehit.DNA*, is one I can honestly market as a No. 1 Songwriting book on Amazon. I doubt that it is still No. 1, as Amazon updates its stats every hour. So how long was I at the top? Even if it was for as little as an hour, it gives me at least one un-manipulated screen grab of dominance. For the record, I was No. 1 for longer than an hour, but not as long as a month. But does it matter?

Note that I didn't go for the impossible. A niche book like *Futurehit.DNA* had essentially zero chance of being the biggest-selling book across all of Amazon, even for an hour. I didn't bother chasing that. I focused on a relevant sub-genre that made a difference in my marketing efforts. No need to sell thousands of copies in a concentrated period of time to accomplish my goal. I didn't even need hundreds.

This is how choosing your sub-genres when you distribute your music becomes important. You need to pick terms that accurately describe your music. But you should also be cognizant of the sub-genre chart where you want to look good. So choose descriptions that you can plan on promoting once you get a good position from coordinating your own internal sales efforts.

Focus the efforts of everyone on your team on these sites, and then start watching regularly for the chart positioning. Amazon tends to have the most impact, so refresh the site hourly and see what happens. Make sure you take a screen grab to document your chart position; you'll want to promote that to your fans later on. The aura of a hit will make them feel excited about being a fan of an artist who is getting bigger by the day. It may also spur them to buy the song, as many people only feel comfortable purchasing what others have bought. Strange, I know, but true. That's why so many people gravitate to sources such as the iTunes chart to decide to buy.

Don't be discouraged if you don't rank No. 1. Even on the sub-genre chart, it's unlikely that you'll be able to get a No. 1-selling song, but that's OK. In your development period, it's good enough to say that you had a top 10 or top 20 release. Getting a screen grab showing you on a chart between two big-name artists is also worth its weight in gold. No matter where you peak on the chart, for however short a time, take that figure and spin it as positively as you can. Almost any story can be turned into a good one.

Finally, it's best to buy your individual songs than your full album. Album sales are certainly nice, but right now you're playing a quantity game. If you can buy three or four tracks on your album, that makes the overall number on the album look good. If you can achieve 100 sales of each track on your album, you've sold 1,000 downloads. If you bought 100 albums, you've sold 100 downloads. Which one sounds better? Not to mention cheaper!

GIFT YOUR SONG

Ah, the act of the gift. Who doesn't like a gift? I sure like 'em. You like 'em. Back in the early '80s, the music business started a campaign called, "Give The Gift Of Music." It even had some cutesy logo; to this day, I still don't know what it was supposed to be. In the spirit of that campaign from days gone by, I too will suggest giving the gift of music.

Go onto iTunes or Amazon, enter the email address of the person you'd like to send the music to, pay the 99 cents, and away it goes. The person on the other end gets your music, and you get credited for the sale. The beauty is that it only really costs you 29 cents per email.

Now, before you go hog-wild crazy doing this, let me offer a caveat. This is especially important if you have a sizable investor behind you. If you have a lot of money at your disposal, you might quickly see that you can gift 10,000 copies, and the end result is only a net cost of $3,000. That's out of reach for most musicians, but it might be worth it for an investor. After all, three grand isn't really that much of a marketing expense if you're looking to make a big splash, and 10,000 copies will get noticed.

What you have to realize is that these retailers are wise to a hack like this and will make the effort to stop it. If they notice that one person gifted that many copies, they will gladly take your money, but they won't report it to SoundScan. The goal of this exercise – spending the 29 cents – is to make sure you can grow your numbers for record execs to see. So it's important that you keep the number of copies gifted to a low figure. I usually recommend fewer than 50.

Perhaps the most important thing about gifting is to make sure the people on the receiving end actually redeem their gift. This is not just because you want someone to actually hear your music, which should be at least be a main reason for the gift. It's also because it won't actually count as a sale on SoundScan until the other person redeems it.

Even worse, it won't count as a sale back to you. Instead of spending a dollar and getting 70 cents back, you're spending a dollar and getting nothing back. Bad outcomes all around.

When you're gifting, focus only on the small group of people you know will *definitely* redeem your gift within a couple of days. Don't send gifts to random people on your mailing list. It may just sit in their inbox and never get redeemed. It's probably also a good idea to alert those you're planning on gifting in advance. That way, they can reply and let you know they received your message. This will also, it's hoped, give you the signal that they will be more than happy to participate in your hack.

Of course, you can gift on multiple services. If you're really up for making this happen, gift someone on both Amazon and iTunes. Have the person on the other end be prepared to redeem twice. They may think they redeemed it once, so they're good. Make sure you explain that it must be done twice.

I must stress that this is not the end-all hack to a hit. Labels, digital retailers and others are wise to people who "buy" their way onto a chart. This is not a smart shortcut strategy, as it'll be money wasted. The key here is just to gain a sales base to ensure that you're not looking at single-digit retail action. I've seen many acts that hype themselves up with buzz, only to find in SoundScan that they've sold 20 downloads. Again, anything north of 100 at least gets a modest nod of respect, and that's all you're looking for at this point. Anything smaller is nearly automatic dismissal, no matter how good the rest of your story is. Spend a few bucks, and you'll have a base from which you can begin to tell your industry story.

This is not the first hack that I would attempt of all the ones presented in this book. If anything, it might be the last. This is probably the one you want to use to put your music over the top. As noted throughout this book, there is a positive psychological reaction when one reaches certain plateaus. Numbers like 1,000 or 5,000 or 10,000 or 25,000 feel really great, both to you and those monitoring you. If

you are just shy of those goals, do what you deem necessary
to get over the hump.

So skip the latte. Buy and gift your download.

GET PAID TO BUY YOUR OWN MUSIC

Now, quite frankly, when this opportunity comes up, you should do a few things immediately:

1) Stop whatever you are doing and alert everyone you know.
2) Promote this idea for as long as the promotion lasts.
3) Send me a huge thank-you note, as this trick alone can pay for this book.

I'm not kidding on this one. This hack is so deceptively simple and brilliant it's almost criminal. Believe it or not, there's a way where you not only can get your sales count up considerably, but also get some of these companies to pay you for the privilege. In the last chapter, I explained how to get your sales numbers up for about 29 cents each. Now, what if I told you that you could get paid *full price* for each download sold, and it would cost you nothing?

At first, I thought it was too good to be true. As a matter of fact, it's such a deliriously good hack that I have yet to meet a person who had actually thought about it, even when it was in plain sight. I'd tell them the promotion, and they'd stare at me dumbfounded until I explicitly explained it. And these are music industry people with decades of experience. Not only can you can earn *free money* on this hack, but also most other people won't do it because they don't know about it.

And do yourself a favor: Please don't tell others about it, either. The only way it will continue to work is if everyone does not do it. I consider this one so special that I never speak about it in public, to the media, on a panel, at a seminar or while conducting a lecture. In fact, you may have bought this book simply because I told you that I had this chapter and refused to divulge its contents. Since I consider this tip so valuable, keep it to yourself. Just tell others that they have to read the book to find out.

So, are you ready? The secret is in promo codes. Promo codes or coupon codes are distributed by e-tailers to entice you to buy from them instead of a competitor. Most often, these codes are incentives such as free shipping, 20% off, or "buy one get one free." However, when it comes to digital media, the codes can offer more value to you as an artist. Here's why:

If a digital retailer wants to give away a free download, it doesn't cost them a lot. So they can say either "Get a free download" or "Get $1 in credit at our mp3 store" and they're really only spending 70% of that. Their purpose is to entice new users to try out their store, hoping that they will shop at iTunes less and at their store more. Considering that "free shipping" can cost them several dollars, giving out something that costs them 70 cents with the prospect that a customer will buy a lot more in the future (or even right there on the spot) is nothing. If they give you a $1 credit, they're hoping that maybe you'll download the new hit album that they have for $8.99 instead of the $9.99 that iTunes would charge. That's a good value, too, but it's not our hack.

You may already see where I'm going with this. When these codes are made available, don't use it on the hit single you've been wanting. Spend it on your own music. It costs you nothing, but the e-tailer still must pay you the wholesale price for the sale. For a "free song" promotion, this is 70 cents of *free* money in your pocket. If you get your bandmates to do this as well, we're talking about a few bucks free and clear.

Not to mention that these songs also count on that SoundScan chart that record companies look at. Since the promotion is a coupon for any item, it's still being bought. It's just that the e-tailer is doing the buying. So now you've got another great reason to utilize these coupon codes to juice your numbers.

Yet that alone is not the genius of the hack. It's that the moment this happens, you must promote it to every single person on your mailing list, Facebook list, Twitter list … everywhere! And often. Don't rely on them seeing it the first go-around. Fans love to do things to support the artists they love. Just be sure to give them the link and politely ask them to "buy" your songs. If you just give them the code, some may use it to buy something else, maybe that new hit single by someone else for free. Fans do what you ask, so plant the idea of buying *your* song. Also make sure you focus people on selecting a specific song of yours. If you have dozens of songs out there, they'll go pick any one of those available. That's not a bad thing, because you'll still collect free money. However, if you concentrate the redemptions on a specific song, you'll be able to show a more significant sales figure to record labels. You need to maximize these promotions when they occur for the marketing value they offer. It's not just about the money you might receive.

If you concentrate on a specific song, you could very likely show up on that site's sub-genre chart in a very strong position. It doesn't matter if that chart rank only lasts an hour. It doesn't matter if you slink back to "unranked" when the promotion is over. Just register as high a position as you can, get the screen grab and spread the news to the world.

Since you are likely dealing with relatively low sales (maybe 100 or so), this is not something that you can really get "caught" at. Not that there's anything they can do. They're the ones offering the promotion, so they can't renege on the deal. Even the lower sales-volume sites are still dealing with hundreds of thousands of downloads daily. So your 100 downloads might barely be a blip on their radar.

The record labels also won't know, because all they see is that final total. So if you can rack up an extra hundred downloads "sold," they never have to know that a chunk of your overall number came from a hack. The important part is that if you successfully implement many of the hacks described in this book and act aggressively when this promotion happens, it could be what takes you to 1,000 downloads sold. That's a number that, for an independent, becomes very impressive.

And, let's not forget, you get *money* for doing it!

In short, ask your fans to do something that takes five minutes. They get your music for free, whether they have it already or not. You get credit for the sale and money from said sale. A focused push from you could mean hundreds of dollars in your pocket. You already spend as much time or more getting people to buy your music with their actual dollars. Why not do it with someone else's money?

Now, these promos don't come up that often, and they don't last very long. Rather than searching for various sites that run these promotions, just make sure you follow me on Twitter or Facebook. I will alert you to the site and promotion link when it appears. But remember, I won't be telling people about this hack. You'll just see a post that says something like, 'Get $1 credit at Amazon's mp3 store." Non-readers following me will think that I'm just giving them a tip for a free download. You will be the only ones who know this is the key to getting hundreds of dollars with the help of your fans and family.

By the way, I expect that these promotions will start to pop up more frequently in the next few years. As competition for even a sliver of iTunes' market share intensifies, these sites need to engage in marketing tactics like this. As they add new features such as cloud streaming, they will also offer these promotions. I don't care who does the promotion or why. I only care that you use it to hack your hit.

CREATE YOUR OWN MUSIC HACK DAY

Hack days are a pretty fun, ingenious way to get new things brewing. True, it's way geekier than I (or likely you) will ever be, but that's where some of the fun begins. Basically, a hack day is one during which developers come together and brainstorm on putting together new things that, it's hoped, have a cool use. This is usually not meant to put together the latest and greatest piece of technology that will change the world. This is more about assembling something fun that people would enjoy using, regardless of the money that could be made from it.

Big corporations like Yahoo! organize these and often spend a lot of money to entertain the best and brightest who attend. Other hack days are loosely developed by community organizations looking as much towards creating networking opportunities as ideas. Either way, they can be as big or small as you want them to be. The ultimate goal is to search for and spark ideas on creating new things.

Just by their name, hack days certainly scream "technology". But must they? Of course not. It's only the spirit and idea you're going for. Maybe it's technology oriented, maybe it isn't. But what you should be looking towards is a common goal: getting your active fans together to come up with cool ideas to make your name even bigger.

How many people have to show up? It really doesn't matter. Every person is an energy source that can help you become bigger than you are today. Yes, the more people who come together, the more everyone can ultimately feed off each other. Still, even if only three people show up, that's three more resources than you had before. Your job is to utilize them to the fullest extent possible.

The easiest way to do this, of course, is in person. Invite people out to a coffee house. Let the venue know in advance you'll be doing this, and they are more likely to be amenable to furnishing the space in exchange for bringing in paying customers. You can always buy a few people a latte or biscotti, but that's not why most people will come. They are coming to help you, and spending $3 on a coffee is no big deal. Choose a coffeehouse that's independent, as you'll likely get more space and better deals. Remember that independent people looking to grow are always more likely to help each other.

You can also possibly use the club that you're going to play in. Work on getting to the club several hours early and bring your fans in early. The club should have wi-fi, because it will be difficult to get everyone connected to help without it. Also, make sure the club has an area where people can all be seated; no standing-room-only here! Take time to pre-plan with the club owner.

Also think about setting up a "virtual" hack day. Use sites like gotomeeting or just a simple webcasting site with chat functionality like ustream. The main thing is to find a conducive place to gather your fans and ask them for their help.

OK, you've now gathered them all in whichever particular destination made the most sense. What's next? Get them to contribute ideas. This will likely be slow going at first, but once you get your fans to open up, you'll probably get them cooking and thinking of things you haven't done.

An obvious place to start, given the name of the event, is brainstorming different tech ideas. This could be developing some code to make sure your music gets recommended more often. Perhaps it's people posting and embedding your video to other sites you've never thought of before. Maybe it's actually creating new videos to promote your music.

The ideation group doesn't have to come up with tech solutions. Perhaps their suggestions are old school in nature, but feel fresh against your music. It could be as simple as a day to promote your artistry, such as a coordinated effort to post on message boards or write-in blogs. Maybe it's a consistent message on Facebook on the same day. It could be many things that would normally be left up to a paid street team who markets your music, but instead is generated directly from your fans.

Be prepared to offer some prizes for the fans with the best and brightest ideas. They don't have to be big or expensive in nature, perhaps recognition may be reward enough. Fans want to know that they are helping and are appreciated. It could be presenting them with a very simple trophy, videotaping it and placing it on the Web. The more they can show their friends, the more important it will be to them. It could be something more intimate, such as a personal concert at their house.

Are these going to be as elaborate as the more professional "hack" days? No – but that's not the point. This is just a name to put on a gathering of fans to harvest ideas on how to spread your music. It's highly unlikely that they would do this on their own, so somebody (i.e., you) has to be the impetus. Maybe it'll turn into a big annual event that every fan needs to attend ... something that gains mythical stature. That wouldn't be bad, either. Most ideas start from something small. If it yields even one good idea that takes your music to a much higher level, isn't it worth it?

HAVE A COOL MERCH ITEM

I love my friend Jaron Lowenstein.

There, ya sonofabitch, give me my twenty bucks. I put your name in my book.

In all seriousness, this guy did enough hacking from 2009 through 2011 that he probably could've written this book himself. Jaron created this one-man band, Jaron And The Long Road To Love, and was determined to reinvent modern country music. He wanted to make a record where he wrote and performed nearly everything on the record. In October 2009, he and I met for drinks after he had recorded the first few songs. In the ensuing conversation, I discussed with him my just-released book, *Futurehit.DNA*, which he devoured with great interest.

Then the hacking began.

After that cocktail session, he returned to the studio and recorded a song called "Pray For You." He was so excited about it that he sent it off to radio stations on his own label. The stations got a very positive reaction from listeners. Jaron then made a video (thanks for the book cameo in it!), and the song just kept getting bigger. He finally cut a deal with UniversalRepublic Records and Big Machine Records. The net result was that the song was a top 5-selling country song in 2010, even though it was never in the Top 10 at radio. Eighteen months after its initial release, the song reached platinum digitally – a wonderful milestone for any artist.

Not one to stop the train or miss a great thing, he did something fun that works on so many levels. He made a cool merch item. Not just any merch item. He reinvented the platinum plaque in a new way that made it accessible to any of his fans. What he did was take the same design of the plaque and make it a poster with the same look and feel as the expensive plaques record company execs hang on their walls. But the kicker was that you got to put your own name on the plaque, just like the real platinum plaques. All for $20.

This great affordable merch item accomplished many things for Jaron. First, it reminded his fans that he had a legitimate hit record, so they had a reinforced message that the artist they love is a hit artist. Second, it became a thank-you note to the fans that helped achieve that sales status. Any fan could have a memento in recognition for the sales goal reached. Finally, it distinguished him from everyone else who only sold T-shirts, generic posters and the occasional piece of underwear.

Today, any Tom, Dick or Harry can produce a t-shirt. Heck, they could've done that years ago. Then, however, you usually needed at least $1,000 to purchase the inventory to take on the road. You could generate nice profits, but you had to put up that money first. Now, you can just upload your design on several sites, and they'll print any number of shirts on demand, sell them for you and send you your profits. Set-up fees are minimal to none.

However, doing something different and cool puts you in a different league. Jaron's creative hack is a great way to persuade fans you're a big deal. That, in turn, makes them treat you like a big deal when they talk to other friends about you.

The status symbol became self-evident in the '80s with the rise of the music video. All of a sudden, it was easy to communicate huge wealth, fame and status by the potent combination of picture and audience. Big worldwide touring star? Rent a Lear jet for the shot of the band disembarking before the big show. Presumption is that you're always traveling private. A Lavish lifestyle with all the girls? Rent a mansion and hire models for the party scene. Of course, you always live the high life when you're not in the studio. Don't all musicians?

Of course they don't! Most musicians don't live like that 24/7, and some who do eventually go broke. However, there was no denying that when artists used this imagery, they often sold more records. Something obviously worked in this scenario, and that something was appearing to be larger than one actually is. As noted earlier, most fans actually *want* their favorite artists to succeed and be larger than life.

So where does this cool merch item come into play? The reality is that there is still a common assumption among music fans that these cool things cost a lot of money. Since they're not a typical item, they must be harder to replicate. They also assume that cool things are harder to come by. Make a "limited edition," and even a fan base of only 1,000 people might snap up the 100 or so items you have.

Don't worry about making a million of the items to reduce your per-unit costs. Make a hundred. Heck, maybe you don't even make any. Come up with the idea and put it on your website as a pre-order. Then, if someone orders it, you make it.

It's more important to focus on the idea. Come up with something that perhaps has never been done before with music. Maybe there's an obscure musician in Europe who did something cool that you can replicate. Or maybe there's something from another industry entirely that you can copy for yourself. Don't stop if you can't think of anything in 30 minutes. When you find the right idea, you'll know.

Make it personal. This can be an item like Jaron's that has the fan's name on it. It also can be something you create specifically for that moment. Maybe it's a one-of-a-kind drawing. Or a specific hand-written lyric sheet. Think of how much lyric sheets of famous songs go for today. What if you hand-wrote 25 of them and sold them in a nice frame? Your fans might want to buy it now at $150 because they love you so much. Or maybe they see the value in it, and hope to reap $15,000 from it when you're huge. Who cares? Either way, you have an easy, premium and unique item to sell that images your song as bigger than it would be otherwise.

As of this writing, USB sticks in unique shapes sell well. How about limited-edition iPhone or iPad covers?

Think of fun ideas that can tie into the name of your song. The potential list of items is unlimited.

Unless you're an ultra-serious doom-and-gloom moping musician (and I assume you're not, because those artists aren't actively trying for hacks to make them successful musicians), you are probably someone who likes to have fun. So have as much fun with this one as you possibly can. Your fans ultimately want to share in that fun, so oblige them! If you do, it will shine through in your cool merch piece. And then you will have won over the fan and earned the right to do just about anything you want.

Even make personalized platinum plaque posters.

INTERACT WITH EVERYONE YOU CAN

I took my daughter to see the Ringling Bros. and Barnum & Bailey Circus, one of Feld Entertainment's many productions. That company also presents shows like Disney On Ice, Nuclear Cowboyz and Monster Energy Supercross. With several productions touring at any given time, Feld has a great deal of activity to oversee.

I certainly didn't expect much when I tweeted the following from my @repojay account:

"Rockin the ringling bros. circus with my daughter"

I was only interested in letting my followers what I was doing with my daughter. I didn't specifically identify any Twitter tags with the circus, hashtags or anything else that would have popped up in an automated search. Yet by the time the circus was over, I received the following tweet:

"@Repojay thank you for "rockin" Ringling Bros!"

Who was this person that responded to me? Clearly he or she worked with the circus, and with that twitter handle it was likely a member of Feld Entertainment. Turns out it wasn't just anyone, it was Nicole Feld, the Executive Vice President of Feld Entertainment. We then engaged in some great dialogue.

"@nicolefeld My pleasure! Very impressed you tweeted back, esp. on a Sunday. I always love fellow execs who "get" social media. :)"

"@Repojay our business is 24/7 so I never turn it off!"

To tell you the truth, I was stunned. For one thing, Nicole had no idea whether I was any sort of VIP. My bio on Twitter doesn't exploit my background. Unless she had conducted a great deal of research, I doubt she realized who I was. She also wasn't responding to a customer service issue. My tweet certainly communicated that I was having a good time. I wasn't spreading any negative buzz, so her communiqué was solely goodwill. It's also worth mentioning that this all occurred on a Saturday morning. I realize her job involved a lot of weekend business, but one would not expected a senior-level executive to respond in such a seemingly random manner, let alone during the weekend.

As you might guess, this interaction made me like the company – one that I hadn't really thought much about, despite having taken my daughter to much of their entertainment. So I started following Nicole's feed. Months later, she announced their new tour via Twitter, a combination of Marvel comic superheroes and Monster Trucks. The inner seven-year-old in me leapt up and retweeted it to my own followers.

In short, that small interaction months earlier led me to promote for free their new event. This is the obvious power of social networking. Yet the key element that you must take away is that she took the time to find me. If you start to develop any major buzz, it is imperative that you look to Twitter and Facebook searches to find every person who may be talking about you, even in the smallest ways.

And as I mentioned earlier, don't just limit your searches to your name or your band's name. Search for your song title. It's amazing that even when people are actively discovering music online, with all the information sitting right there, they often neglect to identify the artist. Don't fall into that trap; look for people talking about your song.

Search for people talking about other members of your band, too. You may not think that people notice a particular band member. However, if they do and the band fails to recognize that fan, they miss out on a valuable opportunity. At this stage, concentrate on getting every possible fan into your universe, and analyze how they got there afterward.

Take time the day after a show to find people who attended. You may have been the opening band, and someone talked about how much they loved the headliner. They may have failed to mention you, but that doesn't mean that they didn't like you. Reach out and ask them what they thought of your show. Maybe they liked you well enough, but were too focused on the headliner. Maybe they got there later and missed you. Bring them into the fold. Send them a link to your music to show them what they missed. Just don't miss out on the opportunity to communicate with them.

    This hack is vital to expanding your reach and the number of people who will talk about you. This is just as important as talking to those fans in the club. If someone comes up to you at a gig, you wouldn't blow him or her off. If you overhear someone talking about your group, you'd probably go up and introduce yourself. Take advantage of the opportunity to do the same thing on a daily basis online. Not only is it easier to find these people, but it also takes less time than those club conversations! The digital barriers make it easy to keep your chats brief.

    You don't have to do anything special with these one-to-one interactions. Answer the fan's questions, responding briefly and politely to their comments. A simple "I'm glad you liked the show" can go a long way. When someone tweets about you (or anything for that matter), they usually stop thinking about you the second after they finish the tweet. They may not be following you to get more information regularly. It's key for you to pick up that conversation so they will be likely to follow you in return. I mean, who wants to maintain a dialogue with someone who's not friendly?

    Let's review the thread of this chapter. One simple interaction can lead to a lot of things: It might start a regular dialogue, in which case you can safely identify a superfan. It could create a connection that causes someone to casually follow what you're doing. This means that when you do something of interest, such as a tour date or a free download promotion, he or she is much more likely to tell others about it. Or it may be ignored, which is OK. That would have happened either way; at least you tried. The people you care about are those who make a connection with you when you reach out to them, but who would have failed to do so otherwise.

Remember, these potential fans are practically screaming that they want to interact with you. Elsewhere in this book, we discuss finding people who are highly likely to enjoy your music. Those interactions are a bit trickier. This hack, however, is as simple as can be. The value here is obvious, as is the importance of doing it.: Person by person, you will be able to build a successful following around your band. This low-hanging fruit is the sweetest and easiest fruit of all.

UNFOLLOW LIGHT OR NON-FOLLOWERS

Social networking is an ever-widening frontier that companies and individual artists are having trouble wrapping their heads around. What's the value of a "follow" or a "like"? Some artists have modest Twitter followings and sell platinum. Others have millions of followers on Twitter and sell thousands. How does this happen?

The reality is that no two stories are the same, and everyone is affected in different ways. Let's look at the band Phish. For 20 years, these guys never had a record that was a top seller in any year. They always sold decent numbers, but you won't find multi-platinum plaques in their cellars. However, few bands could sell as many concert tickets as they did. There was seldom a year when they were not among the top-grossing concerts draws. If you looked only at their record sales, you might not see a success story. But in terms of tickets sold, they were one of the biggest bands on the planet.

When it comes to Facebook and Twitter, their metrics generally carry a similar meaning. For you, it's important to build your numbers to something substantial, if for no other reason than to show that you're in the game. As of this writing, there's a major-label artist with two singles that has fewer than 10,000 followers. Forget that neither single was a hit. What's important is that if *you* get to 10,000 followers, you're doing better than some signed artists. That's noticeable to anyone who is trying to gauge your success level.

One downside of following fans on Twitter who have a high likelihood of liking your music is that they often don't follow you back. In fact, it's almost a given that more than half of those people won't, let alone the celebrities, businesses, deal sites and maybe even @futurehitdna.

The problem here is that this creates a ratio that often looks bad and might even highlight the fact that you're trying to juice your numbers. Having 1,500 people following you is great. However, if you're following 5,000 people, that also means that you are not as popular, because you care to "know" more people than those who know you. In the above scenario, there are at least 3,500 people who aren't returning the love. For the sake of the name you're building up as an artist, you need to unfollow them. As much as I'd like your follow, that includes even @futurehitdna.

If you're unfollowing people whose information you care about receiving, like mine, then it's best to set up a second Twitter account. Use an alias such as @unrelatedpuppy to deliberately discourage others from finding or following you. You could even lock your account to prevent any followers without your permission. The account's sole purpose will be for you to observe other people at a safe distance from your official artist page. If you often retweet information, use an aggregation tool such as HootSuite so you can still observe from one account and retweet it on another.

With those exceptions, you should unfollow everyone else who doesn't follow you to keep your ratio as low as possible. Use a site such as www.friendorfollow.com to find out which users fit this category. But unfollow these accounts gradually. Let's say you just added someone last night, but he hasn't returned the favor by the next morning. Don't immediately drop him. Give him several days to make sure he's had enough time to get to his account and decide whether he wants to pay attention to you. Think about how many days you might go without checking Twitter. Then make sure that's your minimum time between following and unfollowing him if he doesn't return the favor.

When you do take action, don't unfollow everyone at once. That kind of activity sends a huge red flag to Twitter and might get your account suspended as a potential spammer. Better to just unfollow a few people at a time, at random intervals throughout the day. If you've unfollowed 100 people in a 24-hour period, that's a lot; you probably shouldn't exceed that. Keep the quantities small to demonstrate that your intent is to legitimately target market ideal fans, not spam people.

After you've completed this exercise, you should occasionally filter out people you follow who don't tweet. When you follow someone, you're ostensibly paying attention to the things they say. If they haven't said anything in a year, then what exactly are you following? You'd be amazed at the numbers of people you follow who have abandoned Twitter as a platform. They're not using it and wouldn't care what you do with them on it. At that point they're not helpful to you. Unfollow them.

Before you know it, you've improved your ratio to something more manageable. Now you won't have a follower list that's disproportionately low in comparison to the list of those you're following. This, by the way, also helps you improve things like your Klout score, the importance of which we've previously discussed.

While all of the above really just applies to Twitter, think of similar variations with respect to the other social networks. Facebook is more helpful because your band page only focuses on those who "like" you. It has no bearing on whether you liked them in exchange. However, your personal page may be overloaded with too many friends, and you might even approach that 5,000-friend limit. If that happens, then you may not be able to add genuine friends or fans in favor of fans that aren't active with you. Unfriend them before you get to the limit.

Ultimately, this is somewhat of a give-and-take game as you hack your way to a hit. You do have to add people who may not reciprocate in order to, it's hoped, grab their attention. At the same time, you must maintain this balance so that you continuously appear to be a "healthy" hit artist. At some point, you'll likely find yourself hitting some sort of stasis point, where you're adding enough genuine fans to worry less about the ratio. Don't stop culling your fans as described here, though. Your ratio can use improvement at every stage of your development.

SWAP WITH ARTISTS YOU LIKE

If you're anything like me, you're a music junkie. You are constantly on the lookout for the next big, latest 'n' greatest music. You look at the charts, because you certainly want to know what's going on with the most popular stuff. But overall, you're really looking towards the unknown. If you're a relatively unknown musician, you also look at artists who aren't a part of the big promotionally pushed system. You're finding music all the time.

But what do you do about it? I frequently see artists discovering other artists and not acting on it. Maybe they'll post something or give them a quick nod and say something like, "You're real good, man." That's where it begins and ends. This is a missed opportunity, especially at the early stages of one's career.

Yes, I am also the one who says in my lectures and in *Futurehit.DNA* that you have to look at every other artist as your competition. But you also know what they say about keeping your friends close and your enemies closer. To the world, you should be all "peace and love" and friends with as many artists as you can. Behind closed doors is where you implement as many hacks as possible to keep them from drowning out your voice.

It's this outward approach that gets you the most bang for your buck anyway. So when you're talking to artists, remember the important rule we discussed about free downloads: Give it away for free, but don't give anything out for nothing. What you are about to engage in is some swapping with other artists, and you don't want to do your end of the swap if the other artist won't hold up its end of the bargain.

Let's go back to the band you found. You dig their music; at least enough to say it's pretty good. Your first step is to reach out to them and tell them nicely that you appreciate their music. Then invite them to listen to yours. If you like that artist's style, then there's a good chance they'll like yours and will at least check it out. At a minimum, you've motivated one more person to hear your music and add to your play counts, wherever they may be tallied.

Now that you've established a dialogue, start the swapping. Most artists are familiar with the concept of gig swapping. That's certainly a good one and worth the ask. If you have a decent fanbase in town A, and they have a decent fanbase in town B, then you can certainly both benefit from the exposure. But think about how many people truly show up to your live gig. It's probably only a small number of your fans on Facebook or Twitter, and that's to be expected. Not every fan can come out to every show. Not every fan is even within driving distance of every show (though I have seen fans actually fly in for run-of-the-mill Tuesday night early shows).

The strategy is to go to where you can reach the largest number of people, and that's through your social networks. The trading needs to be on posts to check out the other band's music. Ask them to post a nice mention of your music with a link to your free download, and you will post a similar link to their music. The other band may have an audience of less than a few hundred, but that's OK. Remember that every fan counts, and collecting an additional few dozen fans is important at this stage of the game.

A key point the other band is probably not going to know (and you shouldn't let them know, as in the long run, they are your competitor) is that the link has to go to a piece of your music content that is trackable. No movement you initiate with a new fan should be without this. Database acquisition is probably the most desirable, but even boosting YouTube views is good.

Most other artists will send someone to the home page of their website. That will look nice, but it's not measurable. Instead, send fans directly to the free download page so that the number of steps they need to take to get there is limited. The best move would be to make the download the *only* thing they can do on that page so they're not distracted into taking an action you didn't want. Bring them to YouTube so the video starts right away and adds to your view count.

Leave nothing to chance. Suggest to the artist that you'll give them the message exactly as *you* want it written, and they can do the same. When you send it over, use a link shortening service like bit.ly so you can track how many people they send back. This minimizes the chances that they'll switch out the link to something you didn't want. Link shorteners take out the long cumbersome link, subtly disguise the specific content you're sending someone to, and allow you to track the actions. What's not to love?

Be as nice as possible with dealing with other musicians. Remember that you are offering something of roughly equal value in return, so it's not as if you're begging for something. You're simply engaging in a mutual exchange that will, it's hoped, show noticeable results for both of you. If you find a particular artist drove hundreds of fans to you, you probably want to get closer to them.

The key difference is that you will know what to do with said results, and the other artist won't. The other artist will likely appreciate the exposure opportunity you provided. Meanwhile, you will be engaging in data capture, increasing spin counts, and other techniques to boost the public's perception of your artist strength.

The other thing you will be doing that the other artist won't is engaging with other artists on a daily basis. When the artist in Town B participates in the swap, they will be appreciative, happy and glad they picked up a couple of dozen fans. You, on the other hand, will continue to mine the hundreds of thousands of new artists out there in the world and replicate this technique over and over again. Let's say that each band you partner with nets out an average of 20 new fans. Now let's say you are able to engage one band per day with a swap. That means in less than two months, you will have 1,000 new fans, just from this hack.

The potential here is enormous. You'll keep finding partnerships and using them to your fullest advantage. They'll likely never know that you're partnering multiple times a week to grow and grow. Then, when you actually *do* get a break that puts your music in a notable place, you will have made friends with dozens of bands who will be proud to post how their "buds" got some cool opportunity. The awareness cycle then starts over again, and more fans come in.

An advanced Ninja-level version of this hack revolves around direct collaborations. In late 2010, Tyler Ward, a singer/songwriter from Colorado who's done a lot of cover songs, met up with a band from Nashville called The Co. Out of mutual respect for each other, they decided to collaborate on a song. But they did it without ever even being in the room together; they just emailed tracks back and forth to each other.

It didn't just stop with a song idea. They also made a live video together, again, without ever being in the same room. They both taped their respective live performances and just edited it together. Check it out at http://youtu.be/LhHPiAPakYw. The end result was a video that's been seen over a million times in less than a year. Two plus two definitely equaled 20 here.

Once you start with the swap hack, you can probably think of many more on your own – whatever is most appropriate for you and the other artist. It's additive and rarely counterproductive. Just make sure you're always getting something in return; this is not a situation where you can be generous without at least some reciprocal support. Find those mutual reinforcement opportunities and grow your audience on a daily basis with other artists in the same boat as you.

RELEASE MUSIC OFTEN

If you've read my first book, *Futurehit.DNA*, this next hack should come as no surprise. I've been advocating it for several years, and it's surprising that the majority of those in the music business still haven't quite "gotten" this idea. It's especially interesting because most of the people who do this hack succeed with it. It's all about releasing songs more often.

The artistic side of you might be wondering, "How can I possibly put out quality music consistently if I have to increase the volume?" Maybe you can, maybe you can't. Indeed, the quality might be uneven. Even if it is, getting more music out more often usually benefits an artist's career.

Part of it is psychology. If you, as an artist, are planning to stay top-of-mind on a fan site, you have to be visible. Britney Spears did this for many when her every move was covered by TMZ. I'm guessing you'd prefer to go a more natural path that actually involves your *music*. So, instead of concocting paparazzi stunts, you need to release more music.

The great thing about this is that it can lead to more experimentation for you as an artist. Many notable artists in recent years collapsed under their own psychological weight when attempting a follow-up to a successful release. The longer it took for them to release that subsequent album, the greater the pressure there was that the album be fantastic. To some degree, this pressure became self-fulfilling. From a fan's perspective, when you take a longer-than-average length of time to release something, the thinking is that it must be good because the artist spent so much time fine-tuning it. Whether that's the case or not is irrelevant; that's the expectation.

On the other hand, if you're always releasing music, fans tend to be a bit more forgiving. If a song you make sucks, but the fan only has to wait a couple of months for the next one, they can forgive the occasional dud. Not every Van Gogh is a masterpiece. But if your album is a dud after the fan waited three years, you can probably understand why they'd be disappointed.

Releasing music more often also allows you to keep your fan in closer sync with where you are as an artist. Make a tune you're excited about on Friday? No reason why you can't put it up on Monday. Did a song you tried out live become a quick favorite among your fans? No need to wait months before its "proper" release.

The most important thing, though, is that a frequent dispatch of tunes gives your fans something to talk about, and you need them talking about you as often as possible. New releases capture a special place in someone's mind. There's a little bit of dopamine that gets released when someone finds something "new". The more you can activate that feeling among your fans, the more likely it is that they will continue to talk about you.

Think of your own usage of iTunes, as one example. If you're like most people, there are three places you visit most often: the top content promoted, the new releases and the chart. To get one of the top positions, you usually have to know someone who knows someone at Apple. For the top of the chart, you've gotta be a big seller. That leaves new releases. This area is one you can control every time, so it only makes sense to use it to your advantage.

Spotify, which is the hot music distribution platform as of this writing, focuses its discovery on one tagline: What's New. A consumer could go through all sorts of discovery tools through search. However, when you're in the mood to just listen to music but are not sure what to listen to, your easiest options on Spotify are either the songs you already own or what's in their current chart or new release sections. Experts also use the social functions and search, but that requires some knowledge of where to start. The easiest path, which is what most people take, goes through these new sections.

It's worth noting how the bell curve of discovery has changed. Throughout most of pop music's modern era, songs were released and became familiar as they gained exposure on traditional distribution platforms such as radio. They then peaked and either faded into obscurity or became the classics we love.

The gap between fans and casual listeners has widened in the last few years, and that has totally changed the discovery curve. Fans hear about new music quickly and react to it with great speed. This produces much more activity around the two-week "new release" period than previously seen. However, when that activity subsides, their word of mouth fades, and it takes a long, slow push to re-ignite the activity for the casual audience.

You also see this in the way movies are released. When *Star Wars* first came out in 1977, it had no problem staying in movie theaters for a year. Now, more than 30 years later, it's more likely a movie will be in the theater for a month, or even less. As of this writing, only two of the top 12 movies had been out for more than five weeks. In this instant gratification world, nearly everything in the überfan's mind is frontloaded to the new-release window.

So the key is to create as many new moments as you can, to motivate fans to talk about you as much as possible. The more they talk, the more they turn new fans on. The more those new fans get turned on, the more they're likely to talk, and the word spreads. Those new fans, if you inspire them, will also go back and check out all that you've released before. So no real worry about not maximizing the one song of yours that you know is a hit. The truth is that with each subsequent release, the best of your older music will grow, too.

An increased volume of titles also allows for you to generate a much larger number of overall statistics that can be used to spread your story. You can certainly hope that your fans will watch or listen to particular songs multiple times, but they probably won't buy songs multiple times. If you have 500 fans, is it easier to get them to listen to one song 20 times or 20 songs once each? Either way can net you the ability to say your music has been heard 10,000 times, which can be a great stat to have. The path of least resistance is the latter approach.

Naturally, if you're going to release that much material, you probably won't be putting out an album every couple of months. That's the best possible discipline for you at the beginning of your career, because albums are a big, fat red herring in terms of monitoring success. You heard me right. At a time when many musicians should be putting music up online to grow and develop their sound, they instead hole themselves up for a year in an attempt to assemble 12 worthy songs for an album. Waste of time.

Then, you must ask yourself how people will actually listen to it. Let's put it this way: How many bands have you discovered by listening to the whole album? The answer is, of course, very few. My point is that once people discover you, you want to give them more music to listen to that conveys a fuller scope of who you are. Yet when you look at discovery psychology, very few people are bothered if an artist's catalog at that moment is only a couple of songs. It's just not regarded as a negative. Meanwhile, a full album is only experienced by a select few. The cost/benefit analysis here says to stick with singles.

Another reason to focus on songs is that once you have a bigger catalog, those who discover you have a much easier time finding your best material. Once again, look at your own behavior. When you discover a band with a few years of released material, how do you experience it? Do you pick a whole album or do you start with the most popular songs? More people are choosing the latter as it becomes easier to sort an artist's career by popularity in places like iTunes and Spotify.

The truth is that singles are really just a marketing concept. When you release one as a stand-alone song, you are telling the consumer to focus on that song. When a single is in a list of album tracks, it just blends in with the crowd. Releasing songs as singles, even with minimal marketing, actually *increases* the chances that the songs will find a level of popularity. This, in turn, increases the likelihood that it will be discussed and then has some degree of *sustained* popularity. Rethink the idea of releasing an album in the early stages of your career.

Hacking hits is as much about how you position your songs and yourself as an artist as it is about the techniques to get people to listen. You can release the same 12 songs in a one-year period, but there are now strategic advantages to releasing them one a month (or two every two months) rather than all at once on one particular day. Let everyone else pretend the world is still in an album-based mode. You'll gain a strategic advantage when you recognize that times and technology have changed.

PROMOTE PHOTOS

Photos, in my opinion, are underrated. Although nobody really knocks photos, so much attention is paid to the music itself that photos get left out of the discussion. This is a shame because, with social networking, photos play an increasingly large part of an artist's success. How you interact with them could be crucial.

Today, photos are circulated content, passed from an established fan to a prospective one. Sure, many times they are the goofy pics, but most are the run-of-the-mill variety. These fall into two types: The first is your standard live concert pose. The second is your "pose with a fan." Either one of them is just as valuable for building up your hit-making status.

Allow as many photos as you can. The image of an artist used to be tightly controlled, meticulously defined by photographers, stylists and airbrushers. Now, anyone can snag a pic and post it for the world to see. The truth is that people recognize the difference and understand that the glam shots are idealized; they actually *like* that difference. Not only do you need to get over any apprehensions about distribution of the "real" you, you must also embrace it.

Encouraging and fostering the proliferation of your photos will accomplish a few useful things for you. When the photos aren't so hot, it will show you to be a good sport. It will also show you are paying attention to the fans taking the photos. After all, who wants to take these photos if no one is going to enjoy them?

You can take several actions that will ensure you're maximizing exposure for your photos. One is just to repost the cooler photos to your social networks and your website. On Facebook and Twitter, the more you repost fan photos, the more fans will take and post them, and the more people will see you. If they see enough of you, some will eventually realize they need to check out the music behind the photo.

On these social networks, don't just rely on your reposting to get them seen. Make sure that you "like" the photos on their feeds. Many feeds are now optimizing what gets seen based on how many people interact with the content. If you (and everyone else in your band or on your team) start "liking" the content, then it has a higher likelihood of showing up in people's feeds. Increasing the chances of a pic being seen is crucial. So whether it's Flickr, Tumblr, or any other site that forgets an "e", make sure you "like" every photo you find of yourself.

Posting the photos on your website also helps because it brings together a community of your fans. If fans know they can participate in an official portion of your site, they will do more of that activity in order to be viewed of as being a stronger fan. Encourage them by actively updating a section of your site with fan's photos. Don't wait to get these shots from them. Rather, pull in feeds from Flickr, Picasa or other photo sites where people publicly post their pictures.

While you're at it, join all of these communities that place these photos up. Many of them are now social networks in themselves. When Instagram first came out, it just seemed to be a way to put filters on a photo and have it look like a variety of vintage images. It quickly became its own social network when people were able to post their photos to the site and share them. You could then become friends with various people, based on their photos. Support those fans that are actively taking pictures of you. That should, in turn, get them to take more pictures of you.

Smart hackers recognize that this is another great way to get more fans into a master database. You can aggregate a list of fans that may only exist within that photo-sharing site. However, you can then use that list to message them to join one of your other sites. How many times have you gone to see a band, posted a photo, but did nothing to let the band know you're a fan? Probably a lot. So don't let these opportunities slip you by.

Every time you see a picture of yourself on the Internet, don't just evaluate whether the photographer caught your good side. Think about all the things you can do now that a fan has identified him as such. Do what you can to spread the word about that photo and to make sure you have all the info available on that fan. The more you do this, the faster the word about you will spread and the sooner you'll have more people to spread the word for you.

CONTESTS

Big websites often run contests. Corporate marketers often run contests. Radio stations still demand you to be caller number X to win a prize. Even though there are a lot of contest hogs out there in the world, the reason people still do a lot of contesting is because they work.

Now, should you give away a huge million-dollar prize in order to grow and cultivate your fanbase? Not a chance. For one, that would get you into a heap of legal trouble. I'm no lawyer, but I'd be remiss if I didn't acknowledge that prizes generally require a lot of legal paperwork. So stay away from those. (And if you have a million dollars to give away, hire me with that money instead!)

Technically, you also need the legal stuff for small contests, too. However, this is a book about hacking. Is someone really going to chase after you for giving away a prize valued at, say, $50? A lawyer might advise differently, but contesting is an extremely low-risk way of growing your song into a hit.

You know that this is true because you've seen other bands give away stuff and not get into trouble. Basically, just be fair about it, as one disgruntled fan can upset the apple cart. Be sure you post online that family or anyone who works for you can't enter. That shouldn't be an issue, because you'll probably just be giving away stuff you already gave them.

At the heart of it, you really should only be giving away two types of items: your stuff and your time. Don't even bother giving away cash. That's a fool's errand. You want to give away things that have a higher perceived value than the actual cost. When I'm speaking at conferences, I sometimes give away a book. The value of the prize is $20, so it's a fairly meaningful gift to the crowd. The actual cost to me is the expense to print the book, which is far less than that.

The stuff you should give away is pretty straightforward: a t-shirt, a signed poster or a CD. You can even give away stuff lying around your house. That's kinda sketchy to me, but some artists have had great success doing that. Concert tickets are also good, as they help get people into the show. Doing it by a contest looks much cleaner than just handing out tickets and saying the show is free.

When you do give things away, work hard to make it personal, and use the occasion to grow your audience. Don't just sign the poster. Sign it directly to the winner, so it grows the devotion of the fan and minimizes the chances it'll show up on Ebay. Never give away one concert ticket. Who goes to a show alone? Give away two tickets, and then there'll be a good chance your fan will bring along a friend who may become a fan. Heck, be daring and give away four!

Come up with some unique, memorable prizes that have meaningful perceived value, and watch the level of chatter increase exponentially. Rather than give away a concert ticket, give away a pass that entitles the person to a free ticket for life, as I suggested earlier with backstage passes. You can even make it your thing and give one away every month. Thinking about this, this would only be 240 of them over a 20-year period. That's not a lot (unless, of course, you remain stuck in Local Bandsville, in which case it could eat up your door.) Make them non-transferable. Put a picture of you and the fan on a permanent badge. They won't come to every show, but you *will* have a fan for life.

As you do with free downloads, make sure that when you give something away, you're always getting something in return. Asking people to sign up to your email database is a good start. Do a Twitter contest that gives a prize to one random person who follows you. Same thing for a Facebook "like." Do different contests with different prizes on each platform. This motivates your fans to sign up on each platform. That's important, because the number of people following you in multiple places is a key metric that labels and media watch.

If you've already done a lot of sign-ups, how about performing an action? Here's a good one you can do around the release date of a song, album or video that shows a lot of devotion. Ask people to buy the song or watch the video and leave a comment. Then link the comment to your sweepstakes for a chance to win the prize. This will quickly flood the comment boards, providing the impression that there are some fanatical fans ready to strike on the release date. Non-fans will feel as if they should be part of something, too. All for a t-shirt.

Use every opportunity you have to give away something and grow your audience. A real stealth hack that many artists love takes place when you're performing. Ask how many people have access there to Facebook or Twitter. Then tell them that in 10 minutes, you'll give a free t-shirt to one randomly selected person who follows you or posts something about the show. Have fun and make a big deal of it on-stage, anointing the winner a "super fan." or something.

Rather than having someone walk around with a clipboard asking for email addresses, you've instead collected many fans in a fun, engaging way. You can use free download promotions later to get their email addresses. Yet for that night, you can spike up your social network numbers and have a much better shot that the person who's watching you at that moment will know about your next show in town. It's a huge win for all. I typically get as high as a 25% response rate on this idea. All for the few bucks it cost you to print that shirt, *and* it doesn't come across like a huge pitch to sign up for a list.

Be creative, and you'll find yourself growing your social network audiences pretty quickly. Do contests predicated on signing up other friends. Do contests during your webcasts, and do contests when you've got nothing else going on. Give away framed handwritten lyrics or other personalized, unique stuff that references your song. Make silly, unique, cheap promo items to give away. But above all, make it fun.

TARGET
FRIENDS OF
FANS

This hack was one that came to my attention via a Hypebot article written by Clyde Smith. He actually expanded on an idea from *Fast Company*'s Gregory Ferenstein. The idea is simple and makes intuitive sense: The easiest way to expand your base is to target the people who are friends of your existing fans.

The first site that fully deployed this idea was LinkedIn, which focuses on business networking. Instead of just organizing an easily indexed list of people you know, LinkedIn also established a way for you to network with someone you didn't know. Next to each name, they put a circle with a number that told you how many connections (or, in Kevin Bacon parlance, "degrees of separation") you were from potentially getting introduced to that individual. If the person was two or more connections away, then you probably would not go to much effort to work towards that introduction. However, if the person was only one connection away, it was easy for you to find that connected person and ask for the introduction.

Now, when the connective tissue is just one person, it's easy to assume there are a lot of shared traits. You are friends with Person A. Person B is friends with Person A. Therefore, you and Person B are likely to share similar profile traits. With that, an introduction intuitively makes sense. You have no problem asking, and the other person probably has no problem giving.

Expanding this idea to social networking sites is an easy step. Once you have a list of the people who are in your group of friends, you can see who their friends are, as well, and then, it's pretty easy to reach out to them.

There are a couple of ways to reach out. One technique many artists have been doing for quite awhile is simply to ask your fans to tell their friends. Ask them to post about watching a video, going to a show or reading a blog post. It's probably not a good idea to ask them to pitch friends to buy your stuff; their friends won't do that. You should assume that the friends of your fans are unfamiliar with your work. So why would they spend money? If you're asking fans to spread the word, they need to spread their enthusiasm for you. That excitement should not involve a cash transaction.

You don't want to go to this well all of the time. Your fans' devotion should never get burned out. In an ideal world, your fans will be consistently talking about you. In truth, your fans are more likely concerned first with being liked by their group of friends. If they are mentioning you daily and their friends don't even know who you are, then they may experience some ostracism, even if it's mild. If their friends are not mentioning you back, or not responding to those posts about you, then your fans may naturally shy away from telling folks about their devotion to you for the same reason. And if they stop posting much, there's a risk they may not remain as fervent a fan either.

So there sits the classic chicken/egg conundrum with your fans. A fan's friends won't know who you are if the fan doesn't talk about you. And your fan may not talk about you if their friends don't know you. To some degree, your fan has no problem being your first fan in their group of friends. There's a badge of honor in being the tastemaker in the group. However, if the group rejects that fan's recommendation, the fan may distance himself from you. It's hard to be the only one in a group to like something.

You also have a common situation where the fans generally won't do anything unless you tell them to. Of course, if you're *always* telling them to go message their friends, your fans will seem odd to their friends, and they would likely be turned off. Yet if you never ever ask them for help, you won't get any. It's another chicken/egg situation.

As with anything regarding your career, you should be taking matters into your own hands by just going directly to those friends of your fans. Send them a polite message saying that you noticed some friends of theirs were fans of your music, and you want to introduce yourself. Offer some free music, and, it's hoped, you will entice them to respond either through a signup on your website or a "like" or "follow" back.

Remember you are more or less "cold-calling" these fans, so be respectful of their boundaries. Focus on the fact that you noticed many people in their social group liking your music and hope they will, too. Do not mention which specific fan was where you made the connection. They may make that connection on their own, but you don't want to risk upsetting your existing fan by openly using their name as an "in."

This process is less invasive on Twitter than Facebook. Since the nature of the Twitter platform is more open than others, there is an expectation that there may be more outside messaging than with other platforms. In these cases, you may be best off just following the friends of your fans. If they follow you back, then great. If they don't, then unfollow them several days later.

Of course, you can always combine the two techniques in a way that may prove more effective. Your fans don't want to hit their friends over the head. You don't want to be perceived as invasive to your fans' friends. So type up a message from you for your fans to send to their friends. When a fan is unsure about spreading some info about you, it's because it comes from their mouth. However, if it comes from *your* mouth, it might even take on a little more importance, and that fan can feel cooler.

Start the message with something like "Dear Friends of Joe Smith," and then offer nice words. Keep your message short. Make sure there's a call to action – for example, getting something for free. Maybe make it a contest, where the fan that brings six or more of their new friends to the concert gets a special meet-and-greet. Your worst problem would be spending an extra hour meeting fans. That would not be a bad thing, especially if they each brought along six new friends.

Above all, be nice, and encourage interaction on social networks that expands outward from your fans to their friends. The more they interact, the more probable that your messages will show up on feeds. As this occurs, these friends will start becoming fans. Much like fans of similar artists, this is the next best group for you to target. They represent the greatest potential for becoming your next new fans.

For the original Hypebot article, go here: http://bit.ly/n08YxN

DO A SHOW
AFTER THE
SHOW

This idea came from my friend Daniel Anstandig, President of Listener Driven Radio and a partner at McVay/Cook Media. Daniel is an extremely forward-thinking guy in radio, an industry that is typically perceived of as being slow to embrace new music. If anyone ever needed to hack, it's the folks in a business mired in traditions. Daniel would probably never say it, because his business is more buttoned-down. But I can pretty much guarantee that for him to get things done, he needs to be a hacker.

The secret sauce here is to never let your show come to an end. Don't just say good night from the stage and close it there. As noted earlier, if you are willing to spend every waking moment building your fanbase, you will win.

One of the cool things people like to lay claim to is the "backstage hang." No matter how big or small you are as an artist, there's a visceral joy in connecting with the artist after the show. For the fan, the bond that forms is special and often permanent. Now, with Internet connections bringing you to fans with relative ease, it makes even more sense to just turn it on and connect with as many fans that want to be there as you can.

When I was 18, I went to see a singer/songwriter named Peter Himmelman at a club in New York City. After his set, I remember somehow making my way to the basement where the dressing room/lounge was. Security must've been lax then. Not only did I get to meet the artist, but also he was so pumped from his performance that he pulled out his guitar and just started playing more. Right there, for about 20 or so folks, including me. Was I now a fan for life? Ya damn right.

That's exactly the vibe you can communicate after every show. Perhaps you'll do it straight from the club. Open up the laptop and start right in. Recruit a few lucky fans to participate. Let fans in other cities see what those fans experience. That will get them excited for when you eventually get to their town. Some people think that fans get excited when they get a sneak preview of the live performance they may eventually witness in person. However, I think it's the personal emotion that pulls them in faster. Seeing that speaks volumes.

If the club is too loud, take it outside. Have someone bring a portable, high-power wide flashlight and stream it from the back of the club. So you're doing it by the van; that actually lends a certain coolness. Again, your fans in the club will be excited about the bonus experience. If you're not the closing act, don't trample on the headliner's set. You want that band to like you, and you don't want to take beer sales away from a club that may book you again. But work around those parameters and have fun with it.

If coordinating all of this around a club is a bit too much, then wait until you get to wherever you're crashing for a night. A friend's couch, a motel room, the back of the van. Doesn't really matter. It's communicating the experience of the emotional post-show highs to the fans that creates a special connection they'll talk about. Because most artists rarely go the extra mile in this regard, you can set yourself apart from all the other musicians out there by investing this extra time. Not to mention winning over other fans in other cities.

You can do this on free streaming sites like Justin.TV. Or make it a Google+ event. Another option is the site Stageit.com, where you can charge admission for Web streaming. It's not hard to do, and you could even make a few extra bucks beyond what you earned at the venue.

Regardless, make sure you promote the streaming after-party from the stage. Be specific when you tell your audience to post it on their social networks so the world can know about it. Put it on your flyers. Post it before it happens to draw other fans in. The important thing is to do this and to keep doing it. It sets you apart, provides more things for fans to talk about and secures the bonding that will pay dividends as you grow your hits.

WRITE THANK YOU NOTES

For this one last item, I don't really care whether it's considered too "analog," too stodgy or traditional an idea. I'm not even concerned if you think this idea can't qualify as a hack. It is an old idea, but it most certainly is a hack, because most people don't do it. For our purposes, the hack is the work-around that you can slyly do to make sure your music has a leg up on everyone else's.

Writing a thank-you note is the best way to get attention and remain memorable.

Let's start with what the thank-you note is. First and foremost, it is *not* an e-mail, a text message or a quick post to Facebook for the world to see your appreciation from someone. You can and should do all those things at certain times. Here we're talking old school. Put a pen to paper, write down a few sentences on nice stationery and send it in an envelope with a stamp. That's a *real* thank you note.

Why, in this fast-paced world, should you go through all that trouble when digital technology has made communication so much easier? Why is it important to include this in a book devoted to all the shortcuts that today's digital tools bring us? Because it makes an impact, and one that gives you a crucial edge. To be memorable above all other artists, you must do the things that 99% of the other artists don't, and one of those things is sending thank-you notes.

An excellent place to start is with industry people you meet. I'm not just talking about the record label exec that came out to your show, although that's great. But also the manager of the club where the exec saw you play. The sound guy who went out of his or her way. The bartender who was especially nice to you. You want to be booked at that club again, and it's a virtual guarantee that you will if you sent those notes, even if you sucked.

Then there's the blogger who wrote a great review of your music. The radio person who took time out of his day. The receptionist at that radio station. The owner of the studio you recorded in. The intern engineer who edited your music on ProTools late into the night. All these people and more did something small or large to help your career. Recognizing them in a personal way helps ensure that they will continue to do so. Your career can't be built in a day, so you need all the help you can get for as long as you can. Most stars don't drive their way to success; they get lifted.

Think this isn't done by the biggest stars? Think again. Perez Hilton, who has helped the careers of many artists through his widely read blog, counted Taylor Swift among his favorite artists. He would write extensively about his love for her music. Taylor, as we know, steadily built her career and reached a new high in October 2010, when her album *Speak Now* debuted with over 1 million copies sold in the first week. Taylor was at the top of her game. She'd worked for many years to get to that moment and had reached a position where most people needed something from her more than she needed something from them. Yet a few weeks after the debut, Perez posted a photo of a framed Peter Max print of Taylor that he'd received. Inside that frame was a personalized thank-you note from Taylor. It endeared her further to Perez and his audience. And Perez was not the only one who received one of these.

Believe me, these thank-you notes make a huge impact. During one of my first talks on *Futurehit.DNA*, a young woman came up, gushing about how much she loved my lecture. I was happy and appreciative to have made such an impact on her life, but I was unprepared for what came next. She asked to have a picture taken with me. I certainly don't look at myself as a celebrity one takes a picture with; in fact, this was the first time this had happened. I graciously took the picture and thought that was that.

A few weeks later, I received a card in the mail from an unknown name and address. I opened the envelope and saw a greeting card with that photo on the front. Inside was a thank-you note from the woman about the positive effect I had made on the music she was creating. I was really touched. If I see her at another conference, will I spend an additional 10 minutes helping her out? Of course.

Industry people are not the only ones who should get thank-you notes. So should your fans. Not every fan, but the ones who go out of their way to help you out. A three-sentence personal note from you will be cherished forever and ensure you will be remembered by that person for a much longer period of time, maybe forever.

Make sure you thank every fan who's helped you with something substantial. The one who sent out 1,000 tweets about you. Heck, if you can, keep tabs on certain fans and give them a "1,000-tweet" thank-you award. Or the person whose couch you slept on at a tour stop. The person who brought 10 people to your show. The fan who made an excessively large piece of artwork for you or who tattooed your name on his arm.

There are numerous circumstances when recognizing others this way is appropriate. Make the extra effort to get their mailing address, and put it in your database. Few remember giving their address to you, and when they get the thank-you note, it will be a real surprise.

Get in the habit of doing this to the point that it's part of your routine. Always have a box of stationery handy. I keep one right by my computer so the minute I think of it, I can just reach out and dash off a quick note. I don't write nearly as many thank-you notes as I should. But it makes a world of difference when I do.

Kick it up a notch, and invest in personalized stationery. It may seem like an unnecessary expense, especially when you're searching under the couch seat cushions for gas money. Trust me, those extra few bucks are worth it. When a piece of personalized stationery shows up, it sends an even stronger message that the sender really cares. This is obviously what you're looking to communicate, so don't skimp.

What you write does not have to be complicated. Three sentences are enough, so don't over think it with flowery language. The first sentence should simply be a direct thank-you for whatever action you want to recognize. The second sentence should be about how important that action was to you and how much it meant to your career. The last sentence should be about how you look forward to seeing them again and how much you value them as a producer/fan/whatever. Signed, you. Not only is it easy, it doesn't take long.

It doesn't always have to be personalized stationery. I know one artist who buys the cheap postcards of whatever town he's in and sends those off to fans. They're fun thank-you reminders from the road and can be a bit cheaper, since those post cards are inexpensive and postage for them is less than it is for a letter.

Get in this habit, and you'll see new things begin to open up for you. Watch people tell more of their friends about your music. Notice how certain people will rearrange their schedule just to be first in line to hear your music. A simple thank-you works magic. It is truly one of the most underutilized tools available to musicians, and it pays long-term dividends. You may be spending a fair amount per person in the short term, but 50 cents is nothing if those fans spend hundreds of dollars on you over their lifetime, not to mention the word-of-mouth they use to grow your audience.

And with that, I thank you, dear reader, for taking the time to buy and read this book. This isn't a personalized note of appreciation, but I know how much time it takes to read a book versus listening to a song. The fact that you invested hours to read my book instead of doing something else means a lot to me. I hope it's been worthwhile and you've learned many ideas that will help expose your music to an even wider audience.

Now go hack!

ACKNOWLEDGEMENTS

I may be the only person who sat down at my house, in hotel rooms, in airports, and in cafes to get you these hacks, but this book would not be in your hands if it weren't for many important people whom I am blessed to have in my life.

I am forever grateful to have the most patient, loving wife an obsessive music-loving data wonk could have. The fact that she put up with the time it took me to write a second book is a supreme testament to that. I love you tremendously. Now, please read the other sections of the book.

The music business is great since you often get to work with great friends. Jeffrey Green has been one of those for the last decade, as his positive energy and general knowledge continues to enrich my life. When he asked if he, and his wife Lauren, could edit my book, I knew this book would be elevated. If you want to see the best thematic listing of songs that he's worked on for years, go to www.greenbookofsongs.com.

To all the people mentioned in this book, I am thankful our experiences will inform and help future hitmakers. You may not have known you were hacking when you did what you did, or when we talked. You are proof that hacking is all around us!

The overall support from Daniel Glass and Avery Lipman of my first book was above anything I expected from a head of a record label. Our conversations are always ones I look forward to. Change can happen in this business, and you are both proof of that.

The support from my friends at music blogs and publications really made a difference and I appreciate every character you let my work be a part of. So thank you to Moses Avalon (Moses Supposes), Kyle Bylin (Billboard), Lon Helton (Country Aircheck), Todd Hensley (HITS), Bruce Houghton (Hypebot), Bob Lefsetz (Lefsetz Letter), Steve Meyer (Disc & DAT), Mark Muggeridge (Record Of

The Day), Glenn Peoples (Billboard), Paul Resnikoff (Digital Music News), David Ross (Music Row) and Sean Ross (Ross On Radio).

Throughout the promotion of the first book, Michael Laskow of TAXI became a great partner. Seeing the positive faces of artists at his Road Rally is why I write this book. I'm always thrilled that he lets me share my insights with his members.

This book wouldn't be where it is without the behind-the-scenes business aspect, and that is always appreciated. Jaime Heller and T.D. Ruth of Keller Turner Ruth Andrews Ghanem & Heller are an amazing legal team who've helped me on so many levels. Kelley Rivera and Karen Block at Karen Block & Co. continue to make sure I account for all of this correctly. Ian Rogers, Shamal Ranasinghe and Wayne Leeloy of Topspin make the DTC so A-OK.

Finally, my thanks to everyone on my brand-new DigSin team. Together we are making a new impact on the history of the music business. We are pioneers and hackers. Thank you for joining me on this journey.

ADDITIONAL READING

The information here is pretty advanced. I know this only because I also know many people at major music companies are not utilizing the tactics I've described here. My mind tends to work on that level, always trying to be one step ahead of the rest of the business. I also realize that you may need to take a breath and just get the basics for marketing your music in a socially networked world. For that, I have some other books that are worth picking up.

Ariel Hyatt has been a great friend for many years and one of the first ones to grasp the new social world for musicians. With her co-writer Carla Lynne Hall, she wrote an easy-to-read book called *Musician's Roadmap To Facebook And Twitter*. To pick up the basics of these services from a musician's point of view, this is a great place to start.

A new friend is the author Bob Baker. Right after I completed this book, I met Bob at the Taxi Conference where he gave me a copy of his book *Guerrilla Music Marketing Online*. I have to admit, I briefly panicked that someone had beat me to the punch on the exact same book I had just written. While our attitudes towards winning at music are similar, his focus is more top-level. His digital tips provide a great compliment to the Hack Your Hit strategies.

GET FREE MUSIC FOR LIFE!

SIGN UP TODAY AT
www.digsin.com

ABOUT THE AUTHOR

Jay Frank is the Owner and CEO of DigSin, a new singles-focused music company that allows subscribing fans to obtain music for free. DigSin signs new artists to deals that leverage new platforms, social networks and analytics that expose music to a wider audience, building popularity outside of traditional platforms.

Frank is also the author of Futurehit.DNA, a #1 Songwriting book on Amazon and part of the college curriculum at a number of colleges and universities. The book explores how digital technology has changed the way people discover music and examines what an artist needs to make their song more hitworthy in the digital age.

Prior to forming DigSin, Frank was the Senior Vice President of Music Strategy for CMT, an MTV Network. Frank was also Vice President of Music Programming and Label Relations for Yahoo! Music, responsible for all the company's music programming. He was also senior music director at The Box Music Network, label manager for Ignition Records, managed a live music venue, programmed broadcast radio and created two local music video shows.

Frank holds a Bachelor of Science degree from Ithaca College in Ithaca, NY and sits on the Board of Directors of the Academy of Country Music, The Community Foundation of Middle Tennessee and Leadership Music. Frank also serves on the Tennessee Film, Entertainement and Music Commission, is a co-chair of Leadership Music Digital Summit, and is a consultant at FLO (Thinkery). Frank has spoken at such conferences as MIDEM, SxSW, Canadian Music Week, ASCAP Expo, MusExpo, Digital Music Forum, SF Music Tech Summit and New Music Seminar.

Hack Your Hit is his second book.